THE LITTLE BOOK OF

GAA
Quotations

THE LITTLE BOOK OF

GAA

Quotations

MOTIVATION, INSPIRATION, DETERMINATION

Rory Callan

Foreword by

Liam Ó Néill, President of the GAA

MERCIER PRESS

IRISH PUBLISHER – IRISH STORY

MERCIER PRESS

Cork

www.mercierpress.ie

© Rory Callan, 2013

© Foreword: Liam Ó Néill, 2013

ISBN: 978 1 78117 155 4

10 9 8 7 6 5 4 3

A CIP record for this title is available from the British Library

Printed and bound in the EU

FOREWORD

Ar son Cumann Lúthchleas Gael táim thar a bheith sásta a deis seo a bheith agam réamhfhocal a scríobh don leabhar suimiúl seo.

I'm delighted to pen these words to acknowledge this fascinating collection of quotations from numerous legends of the GAA – and others – throughout the years.

Reading through the book, it really is a fitting tribute to those players and managers who've given so much to the game over the years, because it explores just what it means and, ultimately, what it takes to succeed.

The drive and determination shown by these personalities oozes from the quotes and reading through them evoked memories of memorable moments from great games over the course of many years.

In many ways flicking through these pages

gave rise to a trip down memory lane with players we admired, and continue to admire, providing a rare insight into the small difference that separates winning and losing.

I have no doubt that in years to come, when younger generations take our place at the forefront of the GAA, they'll come to realise that the success of our organisation was built on the efforts of people like those captured in this book, and use their approach as a template for future success.

Finally, I'd just like to pass on to Rory my hearty congratulations on this wonderful book and I hope he has as much success as those whose words feature in it.

Rath Dé ar an obair.

Liam Ó Néill

Uachtarán Chumann Lúthchleas Gael

INTRODUCTION

Quotations from great thinkers and innovators can have a profound effect on our lives. They resonate within us and it was this that led me to compile a book of GAA quotations. The quotes in this book give an insight into what motivates and inspires people who live and breathe Gaelic games. Reading the thoughts and ideas of the great GAA players, coaches and managers gives us a better understanding of what drives them on to achieve success, what it takes to reach the highest level of personal performance and why they volunteer their time, skills and talents to the cause of their local club or county.

The GAA has always attracted men and women who have been motivated by a desire to make their local communities better places to live. People who become involved with Gaelic games have a genuine passion to create something positive in the lives of young people.

I hope the words in this book can strengthen our appreciation of what the GAA really stands for.

Since its formation in 1884, there has been a unique emotional connection between the GAA and the people of Ireland. Michael Cusack, the visionary founder of the Association, expressed the enormous popularity of the newly founded GAA when he said that 'the Association swept the country like a prairie fire'. Within the first year of its existence over 1,000 clubs had been established throughout the country, a truly astonishing achievement in an era before radio, television or the Internet.

That bond has strengthened and deepened with the passing of time and, as the poet Patrick Kavanagh shrewdly pointed out, anyone who wants to understand Ireland cannot do so without first understanding the GAA. Take the case of eight-time All-Ireland medal winner Páidí Ó Sé and his description of what Gaelic football meant to him: 'It's in your soul. It's spiritual. If football is in the pit of your belly then it's difficult to live without. Shapes your life, relegates the unimportant, distorts reality and drags you relentlessly in one direction.' For many people in Ireland Gaelic games are part of their DNA; the games are, as they say, 'bred into them' – they form part of the very fabric of their being.

Quotes from footballers and hurlers are often insightful and discerning, but they can be humorous too, like the Louth footballer who, when asked by a journalist if he had a hamstring injury, replied, 'I wouldn't know what to do with a hamstring injury, probably ate it.'

Of the thousands of teams that start training in January every year, very few of them will actually win anything. There can only be one winner and it's difficult to win, so why do it at all? What inspires an individual to keep plugging away at it year after year? For some it's the feel of the ball in their hands after fielding a high ball, or the sensation in the arms after driving the sliotar over the bar. For others it's the silent moment of comradeship as they trudge off the training field on a bitterly cold night. Gaelic sports, in particular, place emphasis on participation, community and tradition, and you don't necessarily have to win in order to successfully pay respect to these three principles. The former Meath manager, Seán Boylan, summed it up when he said, 'Defeat nowadays is too often deemed to be failure. To me failure is the day you cannot do it any more. As long as you are able and can aspire to winning – that is all that matters.'

Think of the iconic Mick O'Connell in the 1959 All-Ireland final. After a man-of-the-match performance, the twenty-two-year-old O'Connell, who captained Kerry to victory on the day, left Croke Park without the Sam Maguire Cup, returned later that night to Valentia Island – and rowed home in the darkness. Here is the poet Brendan Kennelly's depiction of O'Connell returning to Valentia:

The island clay felt good beneath his feet
A man undeceived by victory or defeat.

Clearly for some, being able to compete and excel in the prime of their lives is reward enough.

Most GAA followers will easily identify with the thoughts, insights and experiences shared in these pages, and I hope will become inspired by them. The word *inspiration* comes from the Latin *inspīrāre* meaning *to breathe into*. It is my sincere hope that every reader, young and old, will receive encouragement, entertainment and motivation from this book and that the quotes herein will breathe new life into their understanding of what it means to be part of the GAA.

Rory Callan

There are people across the whole of Ireland for whom the GAA club is all they have – it keeps them going. There are jobs for everybody, from the greatest coach in the world to the person who brushes out the changing rooms and everybody in between. It gives people something to belong to.

Terence 'Sambo' McNaughton
(Antrim hurler 1980–1997)

There is a big element of mental toughness to every bit of hard training. Everybody has to make up their minds that no matter what comes, whether it is long, tough, or plain childish, that it is going to be done without complaint. Those quiet moments when everyone is suffering a bit and will not give in are worth more than all the shouting and bawling that has ever been done in dressing rooms before matches.

Colm O'Rourke
(Meath footballer 1975–1995)

This is exactly where I want to be. I'd rather be doing this here [playing with Donegal] than going for a night out to a pub or a nightclub. This has always been part of the plan. When I was 14 or 15, boys might be out drinking or whatever; when I was on my first night out, one of my mates said, 'Just take a drink.' I said I had things on my mind, that I wanted to be one of the best footballers in Ireland, I said that at the time. Hopefully I am on that track.

Paddy McBrearty
(Donegal footballer 2011–)

who, at just nineteen years old, was the youngest of the thirty starting participants in the 2012 All-Ireland football final

Keep your eye on the ball even when it's in the referee's pocket.

Christy Ring
(Cork hurler 1939–1963)

The joy in football was always in the simplest things, not in the claps on the back and the medals, but in excelling yourself as a footballer. It was in kicking a sweet free or shooting a goal. Setting up a score or out-running a defender.

Matt Connor
(Offaly footballer 1978–1984)

There are 136 separate skills in hurling, so it stands to reason that you can't be good at the game unless you start young and practise constantly.

George O'Connor
(Wexford hurler 1979–1996)

To win in September you have to suffer in January.

Brian Corcoran
(Cork hurler and footballer 1993–2006)

I honestly could see it. Training through the winter and playing in the National League we knew we had a lot of things to work on, but every morning you were waking up you were winning an All-Ireland in the back of your head.

Jim McGuinness
(Donegal football manager 2010–)

Being born a Kerry man and to have been given the opportunity to play for Kerry is a blessing to me. A lot of my motivation comes from walking the beaches in Kerry. Walking along Banna Beach on a Friday and heading off with Kerry on a Saturday afternoon to Croke Park – it's like going to battle and I feel that I've got to protect what I've left behind in Kerry.

Paul Galvin
(Kerry footballer 2003–)

I'm a strong believer in the group principal, where a group of players come together and agree to work completely as a unit in all aspects of the game, but particularly training and pre-paration. Any player who shows himself unable to comply with that is a renegade as far as I'm concerned, and he's finished.

Mick O'Dwyer
(Kerry footballer 1956–1974, Kerry manager 1974–1989, Kildare manager 1991–1994, 1997–2002, Laois manager 2002–2006, Wicklow manager 2006–2011, Clare manager 2013–)

It all comes down to lifestyle choices. What time are you getting to bed? Are you deciding only to get a good sleep the night before the game or are you going to sleep well for the whole week? What sets you apart in this game is how far extra are you willing to go to get better.

Juliet Murphy
(Cork ladies footballer 1995–)

We just get on with the training. We feel if you put the work in the rewards are there and we just do what's asked of us.

Bryan Cullen
(All-Ireland winning Dublin football captain 2011, player 2003–)

on Dublin's 5.30 a.m. January training sessions

An amazing privilege. The commitment, the hard work, the things that you learn from being part of a team. And it doesn't do you any harm outside hurling. You're constantly trying to prove yourself. You learn to take the rough with the smooth. All those experiences stay with you in some shape or form.

Derek Lyng
(Kilkenny hurler 2001–2010)

on the lifelong benefits of playing and training on an inter-county team

Why do I succeed? I succeed because I am willing to do the things you are not. I will fight against the odds, I will sacrifice. I am not shackled by fear, insecurity or doubt. I feel these emotions, drink them in, then swallow them into the blackness of hell. I am motivated by accomplishment, not pride. Pride consumes the weak, kills the heart from within. If I fall I will get up, if I am beaten I will return. I will never stop getting better. I will never give up, ever. That is why I succeed.

Kieran McGeeney
(Armagh footballer 1992–2007, Kildare manager 2007–)

Since I was a young fella I've always expected to be where I am right now. If you don't have that mentality, you're going the wrong way.

Aidan O'Shea
(Mayo footballer 2009–)

While the All Star award is a great personal honour for me, I believe it is also recognition of the way the entire team performed during the season. This award is as much for the team as it is for me. As a young lad, I used to take great interest in who was on the All Star teams, so it really is very special to be listed among the great players of the day. It's a dream come true for me, but it couldn't have happened without a lot of help from a lot of people.

Eamonn O'Hara
(Sligo footballer 1994–)

on winning an All Star Award in 2002

It's all about how you tune into a game. A person can be as fit and as skilful as they want, but if they are not mentally right it can be a big pitfall. You have to be mentally prepared and tuned in.

Conor Lehane
(Cork hurler 2011–)

The GAA has a tradition of being desperately critical, bollicking players out of it, even from a young age. While training with the Na Fianna Under-8 team recently I decided to try out this positive approach, praising the kids at all times, regardless of their success or failure. Usually I would say to the lad, 'No, you didn't do it right, let's go back and try again.' Now I would say, 'That's a great attempt, but I bet you can do it even better.' I was amazed at the results. Not only did more of the children do more of the drills correctly, but they enjoyed it a lot more. They were thrilled with themselves at the end of the session.

Dessie Farrell
(Dublin footballer 1990–2005)

in his autobiography Tangled Up in Blue *(2005)*

Every last cent of this trip has been raised by the players. People forget that the lads are going out there to work out hard, there will be no alcohol consumed. Everyone who is going has to take time off work at their own expense, there are a lot of lads with families as well, so it is a massive commitment.

Niall Carew
(Kildare selector 2008–2012)
on the Kildare team's training week in Portugal

People can be too animated at underage matches. Hurling should be fun. A young lad should go home from a coaching session loving the game and wanting to play more. They should not be reprimanded for doing something wrong.

John Henderson
(Kilkenny hurler 1978–1991)

It must be said that after the Dublin defeat last year, Donegal were regarded as pariahs, they were regarded as the group who had cannibalised the code, they were looked on as the apostles of anti-football, but this group of guys have shown quality. They've forced a re-assessment of how they should be accepted, they've been exceptional athletes, they've stitched together seven displays of power, teamwork and athleticism. Skill, belief, courage and character have been the trademarks of their play. They are worthy winners today, they are deserving champions and from the tip of Malin to the southerly point of the Drowes river, to the hills that balance the towns along the majestic coastline, through the wild wilderness of the Bluestacks, this will be celebrated like no other and fair play to them!

Martin Carney
(Donegal footballer 1970–1979, Mayo footballer 1979–1990, GAA analyst)

on the 2012 All-Ireland champions, live on RTÉ television, just seconds after the final whistle

Be responsible for your own well-being because no one else will. If you're only half right, leave it and get it fully right. You'll play for longer. As I know now, your future health will be paramount to your family's future.

Bernard Flynn
(Meath footballer 1984–1994)

From a young age I have always played at midfield. I suppose the hurling comes into it too. I just love the feeling, especially in hurling, when the ball is high in the air and you just catch it. That's a great feeling. You don't mind getting a rap on the knuckles every now and then; it motivates you to do it a bit more. That's what you want – hard, tough hurling and hard football.

Ciarán Kilkenny
(Dublin footballer 2012–,
who also played hurling at minor level)

To warm up, six laps of the field, which had to be completed in a certain time (exceed the time and you had to make up for it on the next lap). Ninety minutes of hurling training. Then the real killer, forty-five minutes of physical work: ten press-ups, eight kick jumps, six squats and sprints the length of the pitch, ninety yards. Repeat another nine times. A two-minute recovery period ensued, followed by short sprints called doggies. And we did that from the first week in January to the Thursday the week before the final.

Éamonn Cregan
(Limerick hurler and footballer 1965–1983)

describing Limerick's training regime on the way to victory in the 1973 All-Ireland hurling final

I set in place a personal training programme. Fairly primitive stuff, mind you. Probably the most unscientific programme that any athlete ever attempted. Worked for me though. Regularly, I would set off over the Clasach, run down into Dún Chaoin, and around by Slea Head back to Ventry. Fourteen miles of the hardest ball-breaking terrain you can run.

Páidí Ó Sé
(Kerry footballer 1975–1987 and Kerry manager 1996–2003, Westmeath manager 2004–2006, Clare manager 2006)

on just part of his training regime back in the 1970s

This was the greatest game I have seen in my lifetime and I am speaking of all games.

Erskine Childers
(President of Ireland 1973–1974)

having attended his first hurling match – the 1972 All-Ireland final between Kilkenny and Limerick

You enjoy coming up to training and the craic with the boys and stuff. That'll probably be the biggest thing I'll miss, because other boys have said it before, you don't see much of each other any more. You do drift away and people move on. People have different paths in life and the time you play football with each other … basically you spend a lot of time with each other. You're away at weekends, you're living in each other's pockets. You're used to it, there's a wee comfort zone type of thing being with the same guys all of the time.

Oisín McConville
(Armagh footballer 1994–2008)

I wouldn't know what to do with a hamstring injury, probably ate it.

Anonymous Louth Footballer
before the 1957 All-Ireland final

My circuit was a twenty-minute run, sit-ups and press-ups until my stomach looked like a six pack, another run against the wind and then three shuttle runs and ten hill runs. I spent an hour there in the morning and an hour each evening for well over two months.

Liam Dunne
(Wexford hurler 1988–2003)

on trying to get himself ready for his final season with Wexford

It's always a sign that if you can make it to Sigerson you're not too far off it at inter-county level because you're willing to go over the edge, get up at 7 o'clock in the morning and do the training, you're willing to make massive sacrifices and you know, it's a good sign of a character as well if you can juggle that sort of training and still get through college.

Seamus Moynihan
(Kerry footballer 1992–2006)

I grew up taking frees all my life and I remember going to Croke Park to see people like Tony McTague of Offaly, Tommy Carew of Kildare, Jimmy Keaveney of Dublin and later on, Barney Rock, Mikey Sheehy of Kerry, these were people you would pay in to see kicking off the ground alone – it was an art!

Larry Tompkins
(Kildare footballer 1979–1985 and Cork footballer 1987–1996)

on what inspired him to become one of the game's best free takers

I don't need luck. This game is not about luck. It's about talent and will and want and hard work.

Darragh Ó Sé
(Kerry footballer 1993–2010)

Hurleys have always been a part of my life. I love the touch, the smell, the feel, the weight, the balance, the possibilities of a good new hurley. I like talking to hurlers about hurleys, hearing people's theories on what makes a good stick, what to do to keep a good stick. Everybody remembers their first hurley and their first visit to a genuine hurley maker.

Dónal Óg Cusack
(Cork hurling goalkeeper 1998–2012)

Look, I appreciate that anything can happen. Every tournament is so different. But, of course, doubts do creep in and they're the fuel that drives you on. But I would be very much at this way of thinking – I cannot contemplate losing. I cannot entertain the thought of losing. I just can't go there.

Paul Brady
(nine-time All-Ireland handball champion 2003–2012, from Cavan)

If it can't happen [winning the All-Ireland], why did somebody climb Mount Everest when everyone was saying it couldn't be done? Why, when Roger Bannister beat the four-minute mile, did others start doing it in the next two or three weeks? You have to believe. I mean Armagh had never won an All-Ireland until 2002, then went and beat the greatest county in the game in that year's final. They did it because they believed it was possible.

Enda McNulty
(Armagh footballer 1996–2010)

I always practised frees and practised them on my own. The evening before a match I always went out for an hour and just hit frees for that length of time. I could take a hundred or more frees during that period. So then I was mentally right for the game the next day.

Eddie Keher
(Kilkenny hurler 1959–1977)

I always had a positive attitude. One technique I used to help me in that respect was visualisation. Before every big game, as we travelled on the bus, I closed my eyes for twenty minutes and visualised every situation that might arise on the pitch. I always saw myself as first to the ball, turning, shooting and scoring. I never once put the ball wide in my visualisation exercises and that helped me to go onto the pitch with a winning attitude.

Pat Spillane
(Kerry footballer 1975–1991 and football analyst)

There are a lot of people who have had more talent than I have had and have taken the wrong turn; I always had great self-conviction and I think it is really important to have confidence in yourself and don't give a damn.

Jack O'Shea
(Kerry footballer 1976–1992, football analyst)

It's become a tradition that my players respect-fully unfold their jerseys before every game and put them on together as a unit – this represents our pride in the jersey and the work we've done to uphold its traditions.

Mickey Harte
(Tyrone football manager 2003–)

The absence of long-term goals for a struggling team only helps to keep the team exactly where they are. Every team, every athlete needs that vision. There are plenty of examples of how negative thoughts, or no thoughts at all, achieve negative results. My advice is simple. Set goals for everything: for training, for matches, for your season. Set yourself a vision and see yourself achieving it.

Dessie Farrell
(Dublin footballer 1990–2005)
in his autobiography Tangled Up in Blue *(2005)*

God confers gifts in many different ways. In my case the friendship and goodwill that has followed through my life from the GAA fraternity has been astonishing to comprehend. I am extremely grateful to all those wonderful people who after forty years still acknowledge their memory of my short hurling career.

Tom Walsh
(Kilkenny hurler 1963–1967)

As for medals, I'm not a person who likes to have these things hanging around the walls at home. I don't think it really matters how many you have. It's how you are remembered, how you played the game, what kind of contribution you made to the game, the friendships you made over the years, that's what matters.

Jimmy Barry-Murphy
(Cork hurler and footballer 1973–1986, Cork hurling manager 1996–2001, 2011–)

Training sessions, as regards being tough, they're meant to be. I believe you have to train the way you have to play matches to be prepared to play at the highest level. If you don't sample that in training, you're not going to be ready. If that means you're going to meet with supreme skill, fitness, pace, toughness, physicality, sometimes even a bit of dirt, you've got to be ready for that. If you're heading to Croke Park or Thurles and suddenly you're not used to it, you'll very quickly discover you're in the wrong place.

Brian Cody
(Kilkenny hurling manager 1998–)

Ger Loughnane was fair, he treated us all the same during training – like dogs.

Anonymous Clare hurler

Of course it was disappointing to lose those All-Ireland finals, but I still got up the next day and carried on. I still had a life to lead. I love football, I just don't like it. You can't just like it.

John Maughan
(Mayo football manager 1995–1999,
2002–2005)

Several broken sticks, two broken heads and two bruised fingers were part of the afternoon's play, for hurling, the Irish national game is the fastest and probably the most dangerous of sports. It is a combination of hockey, football, golf, baseball, battle and sudden death.

Daily Mail
report on a hurling match held in London in 1921

A nail had come through the boot. I had no choice but to take the boot off. That meant I was lop-sided, so I took the other boot off. Then my socks were soaking so I had to take them off as well.

Michael 'Babs' Keating
(Tipperary hurler and footballer 1964–1975,
Tipperary hurling manager 1987–1994,
2005–2007)

on playing barefoot in the 1971 All-Ireland hurling
final

There was no television, so young and old headed for the Fair Green every evening to pass away the time. Men up to fifty and children down to six hurled there. I often counted 100 hurling. The hurling was hard – no quarter given and none asked for. It was thrilling stuff.

Joe Hennessy
(Kilkenny hurler 1976–1988)

on his introduction to hurling in Kilkenny city

I tell players clearly about the dangers of over-training and the benefits of proper rest. The rising numbers of groin and knee injuries is, I'm sure, the legacy of over-training. Intense training programmes make huge demands and are a form of stress on people. Rest is vastly under-appreciated.

Dr Gerry McEntee
(Meath footballer 1975–1992, now a surgeon)

I'm always surprised when I hear about managers making stirring half-time speeches which provide enough inspiration to keep players going throughout the second half. Matches are not won at half-time and no amount of talk will change that. The standards are set long before that and, ultimately, they are what will get you through.

Brian Cody
(Kilkenny hurling manager 1998–)

No one enjoys a meal more than a hungry man. The level of All-Ireland celebration in Ulster counties isn't just because winning the Sam is a novelty. Gaelic games in the north, particularly in Northern Ireland, are approached differently than in the rest of the country. Political considerations mean that belonging to a GAA club in Newbridge, County Derry, is different to belonging to a club in Newbridge, County Kildare. When being a GAA member could cost you your life, as it did many times in Northern Ireland's troubled past, watching your county win the ultimate prize – or helping them win it – means much more.

Seamus Maloney
in the introduction to his book The Sons of Sam:
Ulster's Gaelic Football Greats *(2005)*

There is an innate disposition in all of us to imagine that everything was better in our younger days – summers were finer, and so on. This belief sometimes extends to a view that hurlers and Gaelic footballers of old were of a higher standard; I believe this to be illusory. In many ways the games are better spectacles today than in the past.

Micheál Ó Muircheartaigh
(legendary GAA commentator)

Towards the end of March I would do a lot of kicking up in the pitch in Killeavey. I take a bag of balls up and constantly kick the ball over the bar. I'm always the first man out on the training pitch for Armagh and I would always be the last to leave. I spend ten to fifteen minutes before and after the sessions working on my kicking.

Stevie McDonnell
(Armagh footballer 1999–2012)

The ten minutes after the final whistle are like nothing else. Losing is desperate, but if you win, there in the dressing room, the lot of ye together – nothing else is like it. Nothing compares to it.

Dan Shanahan
(Waterford hurler 1998–2010)

The GAA isn't just about what happens on the pitch, it reaches right into the heart of the country like nothing else does. It is something that reaches into homes. We are dealing with people's lives here. It's not about kissing the crest or wrapping yourself in the green and gold. It's something more fundamental. It's about blood and soil.

Jack O'Connor
(Kerry football manager 2003–2006 and 2008–2012)

In the week leading up to a big game, it's important to get the body right and rehydration is a very important part of that. Make sure you have your gear right, gather your thoughts, think about what you want to do when you get out onto the field. Then get out there and give it your best.

Colm 'Gooch' Cooper
(Kerry footballer 2002–)

We played a lot of hurling between ourselves. Saving the hay was a great time of the year, as we used the trams of hay as goalposts. The weather seemed to be great that time and there was also lots of time for the hurling. My father often dropped the fork for the hurley and played with us.

Eugene Coughlan
(Offaly hurler 1976–1990)

The subdued manager on the sideline is just as passionate about his team's success as the manager who is causing a storm up and down the sideline.

Peter Canavan
(Tyrone footballer 1989–2005)

Out on the field it's different than we pretend it is on *The Sunday Game* in those harmless interviews. We can all be some kind of gentleman off the pitch, but out on the field on a championship afternoon, most of the fellas have that killer inside them, some bit of badness in them. And if they don't have it in them, they have to have the capability of doing it through their skill anyway.

Dónal Óg Cusack
(Cork goalkeeper 1998–2012)

We have to continue developing our young people to allow them to become the best they can be. The GAA, our organisation, is in a unique position to provide for this talent development in our communities, whether on the field of play, through Scór, administrative duties or just [to] provide an outlet to express themselves in a safe and secure environment.

Finola Owens
(Fermanagh GAA Youth Officer)

When the final whistle blows the feeling that goes through you is unbelievable. You embrace all the players that you've been doing the hard work with since January; you've been running up hills, lifting weights and training very hard together as a team. So to go forward as a team and get results is something special.

Karl Lacey
(Donegal footballer 2004–)

I'm not massive against drink. There's an off season. You're off for a good few months. Let your hair down and enjoy it. But if you're playing in front of 50,000 people, you have to be in the best possible shape you can be in.

Davy Fitzgerald
(Clare hurling goalkeeper 1990–2008, Waterford hurling manager 2008–2011, Clare hurling manager 2011–)

It's not possible to put into words what an All-Ireland medal would mean for me and this Dublin team. It's the holy grail. It's why you start playing football when you are four, it's why you train hard, take the ice baths and make all the sacrifices. You dream of getting the chance to win that medal.

Bernard Brogan Jnr
(Dublin footballer 2006–)

Nerves are massive. You have to have them. Doesn't matter whether it's your first final or your fifth, the time to start worrying is if you're in the warm-up and you're not nervous. I always thought of them as the ten-yard nerves. If I went out for a league game in March and tried to kick the ball over the bar from fifty yards, the ball could hop twice before it got to the posts. At three o'clock on All-Ireland final day? That ball was making the distance with plenty to spare. You could jump that few inches higher and run those few yards faster. That comes from those nerves.

Darragh Ó Sé
(Kerry footballer 1993–2010)

There are some things in life that are more important than money and the GAA is one of them.

Joe Brolly
(Derry footballer 1990–2001 and football analyst)

I saw Christy Ring doing something in Croke Park one day that no one else would do. We were playing Connacht, the full back was after giving him a belt across the head and he was lying on his back on the ground, being attended to by the two Knights-of-Malta men. We were playing into a gale, into the Hill 16 end. I was after moving out to the halfway line, when Philly Grimes of Waterford got the ball and drove it into the Connacht goal. Ring was still on the ground at this stage, panned out. He never took his eye off the ball though, and all the while he was following the play. He jumped up, grabbed the ball, turned, stuck it in the net, and fell back down on his back again. I was after following up and he looked up at me. 'Doyle,' he said, 'you never did that!'

Jimmy Doyle
(Tipperary hurler 1957–1973; football coach with Derry, Cavan, Tyrone, Monaghan and Meath)

The coach must have the right attitude towards his work and the game generally. He must have a proper sports philosophy, where the spirit of sportsmanship is given pride of place. The mental approach towards winning and losing must be conditioned with this spirit of sportsmanship. Players must be taught to accept defeats and victories with the same good grace. In victory they must have the sympathetic and encouraging word for the defeated, and in losing must congratulate the victors with the spirit of sincerity and manly acceptance of defeat that is the hallmark of good sportsmanship.

Dr Éamon O'Sullivan
from his seminal coaching book The Art and Science of
Gaelic Football *(1958)*

It's great to be a professional and getting to play sport but, for me, pulling on the Sydney Swans jumper was just not the same as pulling on a Rathvilly or Carlow jersey. There is a lot to be said for lining out beside your brothers and the friends you've grown up with. For me it was just not the same in Australia.

Brendan Murphy
(Sydney Swans footballer 2007–2009, Carlow footballer 2010–)

on his decision to leave his promising Aussie Rules career and return to play Gaelic football with his club and county

A hurley is also a weapon and no matter how good or bad you are, you can end a fella's career with one swing. There's a restraint there, a discipline that you mightn't get in other games, but it has to be there.

Ray Cummins
(Cork hurler 1968–1982)

The size of the hurling field did not bother us. I played hurling in a room and I played it with the goalposts a mile apart. We made little of stone walls and roads and other obstacles. We played with sticks without bosses and we played with hurleys. We played when there were only two of us and we played when there were more than sixty of us locked in deadly combat.

Michael Cusack
(founder of the GAA)

on the enthusiasm for hurling during his youth in 1850s Clare

Defeat nowadays is too often deemed to be failure. To me failure is the day you cannot do it any more. As long as you are able and can aspire to winning – that is all that matters.

Seán Boylan
(Meath football manager 1983–2006)

Yet there is one other attribute that is absolutely necessary if real progress is to be achieved and that is hunger. A team's appetite for success can be quickly gauged from players' body language during games and often opponents, sensing chinks in their armour in this context, can over-power them without necessarily playing with greater poise and panache.

Joe Kernan
(Armagh footballer 1971–1988, Armagh football manager 2001–2006)

I'm a different man on the field of play or on the sideline. The game takes over and that's it. There's no holding back. The game gets so much inside of me when I'm in the middle of the action.

Billy Morgan
(Cork hurler, footballer 1966–1981 and Cork football manager 1986–1996, 2003–2007)

A Kerry footballer with an inferiority complex is one who thinks he's just as good as everybody else.

John B. Keane
(author, playwright and Kerryman)

The biggest thing for me was to be able to walk off the pitch and have my head held high. And down deep, to know that I gave it everything I could for my team and for my teammates. I tried to do that, and then there's no point in going round sulking about it. You gave it your best shot and now it's time to spend a bit of time with your wife or your girlfriend or your friends and have a bit of fun. I always try to have that sort of a situation where, once it's over, it's over.

Liam McHale
(Mayo footballer 1988–2001)

I think a Kerry All-Ireland won against Dublin is worth two others to them and certainly it's worth three to us to beat Kerry in the final. I enjoy Kerry people and the craic that goes on between Dubliners and Kerry people very much. We have, I think, an almost unique relationship.

Kevin Heffernan
(Dublin football manager 1973–1976 and 1979–1983)

Winning the game is what it has all been about, but not at all costs. I've always felt that I can outplay my opponent. If I have to resort to bullying him or intimidating him then I've been defeated, irrespective of the result of the game.

Brian Corcoran
(Cork hurler and footballer 1993–2006)
who was never sent off in a game in his career

Journalist: How do you feel?

David Beggy: F****d.

Journalist: Do you feel anything printable?

David Beggy: How about bollixed?

> *Interview in the Meath dressing room just moments after Beggy had scored the winning point against Dublin in the last minute of the dramatic four-match saga which gripped the whole country in the summer of 1991*

A championship game is like a bungee jump that lasts for seventy minutes. The enjoyment only comes when you're unstrapped and you look back up and say, 'I did that. How the f**k did I do it?'

Declan Darcy
(Leitrim footballer 1988–1998, Dublin footballer 1998–2002)

Whenever a team loses, there's always a row at half time, but when they win, it's an inspirational speech.

John O'Mahony
(Leitrim football manager 1992–1996, Galway football manager 1997–2004, Mayo football manager 1987–1991, 2006–2010)

The figure seated on a broad boulder at the foot of a round tower was that of a broad-shouldered deep-chested strong-limbed frank-eyed red-haired freely freckled shaggy-bearded wide-mouthed large-nosed long-headed deep-voiced bare-kneed brawny-handed hairy-legged ruddy-faced, sinewy-armed hero.

James Joyce
(novelist)

describing the Citizen in the Cyclops episode of
Ulysses. *The Citizen was widely believed to be based on larger-than-life Clareman, Michael Cusack, the founder of the GAA*

There is no mystery about the whole thing. If you're going to be taking part in the league and championship every year there's no point in taking part unless you are totally committed to being as successful as you possibly can be – because the feeling you get from winning certainly beats the feeling you get from not winning.

Brian Cody
(Kilkenny hurling manager 1998–)

We know the old story of meeting fire with fire and we know that Kilkenny will come out blazing into the game today. But my attitude would be meet fire with an inferno and that's what Galway will have to do today.

Ger Loughnane
(Clare hurler 1973–1987, Clare hurling manager 1994–2000, Galway manager 2006–2008)

before the 2012 All-Ireland final replay

Looking back now, I was really fortunate to have played with the teams and the players that I did, in my club, St Joseph's, and with Clare. I owe an awful lot to those players in my club and with the county and to all the trainers and coaches who gave their time to improve us as players.

Seán McMahon
(Clare hurler 1994–2006)

The first night I went to training, twelve people trained. When we got to the All-Ireland final, we needed two changing rooms to hold the players that were on the panel.

Ross Carr
(Down footballer 1986–2000)

on Down's progress during 1992, the year the county captured their first All-Ireland title since 1968

Winning the All-Ireland Club Championship in 2006 [with Donaghmoyne] was my most memorable moment in football. To win an All-Ireland Senior Club with players you've been playing with since you were nine, ten or eleven, coming up through the ages together, is something special.

Sharon Courtney
(Monaghan ladies footballer 2006–)

Girls are very skilful players. A lot of my companions on the men's scene wouldn't understand it, unless you go actually to a game and watch them play live. They're really really skilful.

John Divilly
(Galway footballer 1998–2003, Kildare footballer 2004–2007, Kildare ladies football manager 2012–)

It was not hard for me ever to get anybody to play hurling or football with. I was the youngest of fifteen and when a goalkeeper was needed I would have no choice but to go in goal. The games were tough and no prisoners taken. I suppose this stood to all of us during our playing days.

Damien Fitzhenry
(Wexford hurling goalkeeper 1993–2010)

This whole outlook Jim [McGuinness] has on football, you can apply it to life or anything like that. What you put in you're going to get out. We are down there dogging ourselves every single night we go to training. And the results are showing. You can apply that to anything at all.

Éamon McGee
(Donegal footballer 2004–)

For the week coming up to a big championship match you're hydrating, drinking plenty of fluids, loads of water, eating healthy, resting as much as you can and trying to relax and follow your normal daily routine.

Cora Staunton
(Mayo ladies footballer 2000–)

No matter what game you play in the world, if you think you don't have to work you are never going to get the ball. You have to be able to work and in this day and age that's what it's all about. They all have the skills and they all have the ability, and they all can score and defend, but I think when you are at the top level in inter-county hurling then you have got to be able to work extremely hard.

Anthony Cunningham
(Galway hurling manager 2011–)

I work off four words: Commit, focus, believe, achieve. The hardest thing is the commitment. But these players made the commitment. They really focused on the commitment that they made. The third one is belief and when you put the three together, in my opinion, the by-product of that is achievement.

Jim McGuinness
(Donegal football manager 2010–)

The GAA might have turned into a sports organisation and nothing else. The extraordinary growth of this one humble enough association is really a measure of the vitality that lies inert in the common people. In spirit as in its achievement the GAA is not only unique but astonishing.

Daniel Corkery
(historian and writer)

The art of kicking, therefore, is one of the most important of the various skills required for every first-class footballer. It should occupy an important place in coaching and training sessions. All players should practice regularly to attain full efficiency in every type and method of kicking.

Dr Éamon O'Sullivan
taken from his seminal coaching book The Art and Science of Gaelic Football *(1958)*

The GAA is like having a family and the heart of the family is the club. The GAA club moulds young men and women into the kind of people they are going to be. It's like a home. You make friends and you make foes. It is all part of life.

Terence 'Sambo' McNaughton
(Antrim hurler 1980–1997)

Somebody has said that no man can adequately describe Irish life who ignores the Gaelic Athletic Association, which is true in a way, for football runs women a hard race as a topic for conversation.

Patrick Kavanagh
(poet and Monaghan man)
from his famous essay 'Gut Yer Man'

You might be the best footballer in the world, but if you're cramping up in the last ten minutes of a game you're no good to anyone, you'll be hauled off. It's absolutely critical that you get your hydration right, that you get your nutrition right, eating the right foods, drinking enough, and all at the right time.

Dessie Dolan
(Westmeath footballer 1999–)

It's better as a player, but when you are forty-four and two stone overweight and going slow, winning [an All-Ireland] as a manager isn't bad.

Páidí Ó Sé
(Kerry footballer 1975–1987, Kerry football manager 1996–2003, Westmeath manager 2004–2006, Clare manager 2006)

It is that sense of allegiance to something permanent and enduring that has always been our strength. Our rules derive not only from a desire to organise health-giving exercise, but from a determination to defend national values, traditions and aims. That is what has given an enduring vitality to the work of the Gaelic Athletic Association. This is the force which has forged the links that bind our members. At all times we shall continue to guard our pastimes that have enriched the national life.

Dan O'Rourke
(GAA President 1946–1949)

A player's mind needs to be at rest or else he is using up the nervous energy needed at 3.30 next Sunday. The man who goes into battle has to be like a giant fountain, with everything from the outside gently washing off him.

Colm O'Rourke
(Meath footballer 1975–1995)

The game owns you. It's unbelievable. You're in that bubble and you don't see things that straight. When you want to win like that, you'll do anything to get it. You'll believe whatever you need to believe. Whatever floats your boat to get you that performance next Sunday, that's what you'll believe in. Whether it's running up Mount Everest, eating two oranges, whatever it takes.

Seán Óg Ó hAilpín
(Cork hurler 1995–2012)

At that time, I used to go out kicking ball in the morning all the time. I would always get up every Sunday morning at 6 o'clock and go out and kick ball. I'd go out to Fintra, the pitch down the road from me, and go and kick football for about an hour, an hour and a half, then come back and shower and go to mass. That was my regime that time when I started out early.

Martin McHugh
(Donegal footballer 1981–1994)

The biggest thrill I got playing the game was going into a big group of players and winning the ball in the air after a big kick.

Larry Tompkins
(Kildare footballer 1979–1985 and Cork footballer 1987–1996)

Billy Rackard's block on one of the Limerick forwards when he had a clear shot on goal is something I'll never forget. His hurl was knocked from his hands and with no time to pick it up he went in and blocked the Limerick man's stroke with his bare hands. That one act of courage was the winning of the game.

Martin Codd
(Wexford hurler 1949–1965)

describes the last minute of the 1958 league final between Wexford and Limerick

Of course you get nervous when you're coming up to the match and if you're not nervous it's a sign that you don't care.

Damien Hayes
(Galway hurler 2004–)

The key to coming back from an injury is not thinking about it when you're out on the field. Once you run across that white line you have to convince yourself that everything is 100 per cent so that you play naturally.

Tadhg Kennelly
(Kerry footballer 2009 and Australian Rules footballer with the Sydney Swans 2001–2011)

in his book Unfinished Business *(2009)*

Attitude is tremendously important in chasing success – in any field of endeavour. That's why I believe talent alone will get you very little in this world.

Jim Stynes
(Dublin minor footballer 1983–1984 and Australian Rules footballer with Melbourne Football Club 1987–1998)

The whole heart of the organisation will be gone if the games go professional. I never want to see that. If you haven't the heart in the association, you have nothing.

D. J. Carey
(Kilkenny hurler 1988–2007)

Jimmy said, 'I'm handing out your jerseys. Number one, Dónal Óg Cusack.' I mean, it was like Christy Ring handing you your jersey. You were thinking, this guy is one of the all-time greats, and he's handing me my jersey. There's an onus on me to perform today. I owe it to him.

Seánie McGrath
(Cork hurler 1997–2003)

on the inspiring effect Jimmy Barry-Murphy had on the Cork players before the 1999 All-Ireland hurling final

If anyone wants to know about Irish culture or what it means to be Irish, they should come to Croke Park on All-Ireland final day.

Jarlath Burns
(Armagh footballer 1988–2001)

I noticed when they were coming out of the tunnel, they were hitting the ball at the goal, which was eighty, eighty-five metres away out at an angle. I was thinking, why make your first experience in Croke Park a negative one? I told them to jog up towards the goal and to go as far as the twenty-one-metre line if they had to, but to stick their first shot over the bar. At least that way their first experience would be positive.

Donal O'Grady
(Cork hurling manager 2002–2004)

I suppose from around age eight or nine I was out on the farm and there were lots of things you could target practice on. I used to rob an old tyre from the silage pit from Dad and hang it up and hit the ball at it.

Joe Canning
(Galway hurler 2008–)

I suffered a bit here [when first attending St Kieran's College] as I was not up to the standard of a lot of the other kids and was well down the pecking order in hurling terms. But it did teach me to work hard and by the time I had left Kieran's, I felt I had done this – with an All-Ireland Colleges medal to boot.

Henry Shefflin
(Kilkenny hurler 1998–)

Football talk is about eternal things: style, courage, determination, speed, cunning, complacency, waste, recklessness, the ability to work, intelligence, victory, defeat, renewal.

Brendan Kennelly
(poet and Kerryman)

It was a great day, a great experience. The All-Ireland final will beat any World Cup final or European final trust me. Not that I've been to a World Cup final, but I've been to a few Champions League finals. It's about local pride, that's what the GAA is – people representing their parishes and the streets where they grew up. Gaelic football in Ireland is different. They all come from their local parishes. They don't move clubs when they get fed up. They represent the people they're brought up with.

Roy Keane
(soccer player with Manchester United 1993–2005 and Ireland 1991–2006)

What does a player need to be successful? From my experience of nearly twenty years, with Na Fianna and Dublin, my list is as follows: discipline, respect, confidence, courage, enthusiasm, perseverance, leadership, belief, responsibility, self-control, gratitude, tenacity, diligence, humility, poise, consistency, competitiveness, trust, loyalty, patience, initiative, intelligence, talent and maturity.

Dessie Farrell
(Dublin footballer 1990–2005)

in his autobiography Tangled Up in Blue *(2005)*

If you keep hurling into October–November every year, it shortens the time you're without a hurley in your hand. It makes sense. If you puck a thousand balls and another lad pucks a hundred, then you're going to be better.

Mark Landers
(Cork hurler 1998–2002)

Playing schools matches for Gowran brought us into contact with other boys and teachers from around the county. Schools like Kilkenny CBS National School, Thomastown NS etc. The teachers in these schools are the secret heroes of Kilkenny hurling, men who have put in hours upon hours of work over the years. And that's where the road to Croke Park begins: in the national schools of the county. The debt that Kilkenny hurling owes to the teaching profession is immense.

Charlie Carter
(Kilkenny hurler 1994–2003)

It's the best craic you'll ever have after a hard day's work or whatever. The craic in the dressing room is what it's all about. You train hard and then the craic starts again.

Ken McGrath
(Waterford hurler 1996–2011)

If the pitch had a moat around it – as in some stadiums in South America – the delirious people in orange and white would have walked on water.

Con Houlihan
(sports journalist)

on the reaction of the Armagh supporters to their first All-Ireland title win in 2002

Looking at your opposite number and knowing deep down with honesty that you've done more over the past nine months than him; that you've made more sacrifices; that [means] you'll have that small but ever so significant psychological advantage going into the last five minutes.

Seán Kelly
(international cyclist)

addressing the Waterford hurling team in 2007

In hurling or football, why do you enter the All-Ireland? To win it, not to have fun or to come second. You might enter knowing that it's going to be difficult to win it this year, but it's a progression to winning it in four years' time; to start putting the pieces into place, like the fitness, and accumulate that over three, four or five years until you are in a position to win it. So you enter an All-Ireland to win it either now or in the near future.

Gerry Fitzpatrick
(Waterford hurling coach 2005)

It was for me a great pleasure to have played so much football with so many great friends. This for me was the real victory. Travelling the country, meeting so many like-minded people who just loved the game, was indeed a wonderful thing.

Maurice Fitzgerald
(Kerry footballer 1988–2001)

When you think of people like Colm Cooper, Henry Shefflin, Cora Staunton and Bernard Brogan, they are the marquee names within the GAA at present, but they would never have been able to make it to the top without the unrivalled dedication from all of their coaches from a very early age. It is the volunteers throughout all of our clubs that ultimately make the superstars out of our players. I can remember all of my managers from every age group I played at, and each and every one of them taught me something that has always stuck. That could be anything from toe-tapping to making space.

Steven McDonnell
(Armagh footballer 1999–2012)

The spine of Irishness consists of thousands of people voluntarily spending hundreds of thousands of hours a year coaching young people and working for their local clubs, all because they love their sport, the good it does for their communities, and the good it does Ireland. It is that sense of locale which gives the GAA its very rootedness in Irish life.

Kevin Myers
(journalist, writing in The Irish Times *in 2002)*

You should play every game as if it's your last, but make sure you perform well enough to ensure it's not.

Jack Lynch
(Cork footballer and hurler 1936–1950,
Taoiseach 1966–1973, 1977–1979)

At training we used to play a lot of twelve- or thirteen-a-side matches and they were hell-for-leather. Brian McEniff would referee them and a lot of nights he would have to blow them up because of the fights. They were ferocious and not an inch was given. Players were trying to get their places.

Noel Hegarty
(Donegal footballer 1991–2002)

on the Donegal team's preparation in the weeks before the 1992 All-Ireland final

War without bullets.

Ger Loughnane
(Clare hurler 1973–1987, Clare hurling manager 1994–2000, Galway manager 2006–2008)

pre-match comment on the 1998 Munster hurling final between Clare and Waterford

Our world: Winning, Discipline, Professionalism, Team Spirit, Positivity, Performance, Taking Responsibility, Setting Standards.

Their World: Losing, Fighting, Blaming others, Playing for oneself not the team, Relying on luck, Bringing down others to their level.

Sign displayed in the Cork dressing room before their clash with Waterford in the 2006 Munster final

Personal pride is a good thing. The team is number one, but you're out there on the field and you've a job to do. I've to mark a fella and he's my business. Sometimes when we win games and I play terribly I feel like it's a loss. You go out the next day and try to buck up your performance.

Tomás Ó Sé
(Kerry footballer 2000–)

There is just a satisfaction that comes with winning games. Winning games, no matter what way you win them, still gives you the same sense of satisfaction, whether you won them by 500 points or whether you win by two, it does not matter a bit.

Michael Murphy
(Donegal footballer 2007–)

Tipperary player: 'By God Christy, We'll have to shoot you.'

Christy Ring: 'Oh sure ye might as well, ye've tried everything else.'

Exchange between Christy Ring and a Tipperary player after Ring had scored the winning point in a feisty league encounter

Sport and recreation are only a part of that story. GAA helps to instil in us a sense of community, identity and pride. It is the lifeblood of many different communities throughout the country. Every town and village has a Gaelic club that has provided sport and physical activity for generations of youth over the past 127 years.

Enda Kenny TD
(Taoiseach 2011–)

As you think, so you shall be. That is the core philosophy I have carried on every step of this journey. Our destiny is based on how we react to life. Take that sentiment on board, and gradually we can find we have much more control of our destiny than we might once have thought.

Mickey Harte
(Tyrone football manager 2003–)

I remember going out onto the pitch, getting to the halfway line and looking up to see a wall of red and black. It was the most amazing sight I have ever seen. I remember walking around in the parade saying, 'there is no way we are going to lose'. It wasn't putting pressure on you. It carried you.

Ross Carr
(Down footballer 1986–2000)

on the psychological advantage the Down supporters gave the team during the 1991 All-Ireland final

Indiscipline comes with not being fit – when you're not fit, you are going to be narky and foul.

Peter Queally
(Waterford hurler 1993–2003)

He was a man in constant evolution: testing, studying, learning, revising, reflecting, reviewing. He kept diaries of his performances in training and matches years before it ever became innovative. If you were talking to him, his neck would be stretching out, making sure he was absorbing every syllable of information. His eyes were totally focused on you. If somebody ran between you while you spoke, he wouldn't even notice. It was total focus. Precise, intense focus.

Mickey Harte
(Tyrone football manager 2003–)

on Cormac McAnallen, the Tyrone footballer who died suddenly at the age of twenty-four in 2004

If you're sloppy and careless with players it's a guarantee that you'll get sloppiness and carelessness back.

Brian Cody
(Kilkenny hurling manager 1998–)

When I was younger I wouldn't have been the most promising of any of the lads. Even at seventeen I would never have been the standout player with the sides I played on. Despite never really catching anyone's attention, becoming a county player was something that was always in my head. For some reason, with no evidence to support it, I always thought I could make it. I was probably the only one to believe it, and I genuinely did believe it.

Darragh Ó Sé
(Kerry footballer 1993–2010)

Hell hath no fury like an Ulster football supporter.

Joe Brolly
(Derry footballer 1990–2001
and football analyst)

If you think that by intellectualising coaching you can make kids better, you're wrong ... Most top hurlers honed their skills against a wall.

Liam Griffin
(Wexford hurling manager 1995–1996)

The best Gaelic footballers and hurlers in Ireland are deathly serious about their careers. They, like we all did, are putting their lives, their business careers and their families on hold for ten years or more in the great number of cases in order to achieve something. When I first became a 'Countyman' I remember still the magical sense of pride I felt and which my family shared. It was all-consuming. I was prepared to build my life around my life as a 'Countyman'.

Liam Hayes
(Meath footballer 1983–1996)

in his autobiography Out of Our Skins *(1992)*

I remember the 1960 Munster final with Cork in Thurles. That was the most titanic battle we were ever in. I remember playing that day on Paddy Barry. We did the honourable thing. When we had a row during the match we put the hurleys down, had a boxing match, got finished with it, picked up our hurleys again and went away about it. I think the crowd loved it.

John Doyle
(Tipperary hurler 1949–1967)

Out of politeness I asked Eoin Mulligan if he wanted to take it. He said, 'I don't mind.' That made up my mind. I had to hit this.

Peter Canavan
(Tyrone footballer 1989–2005)

on the seconds before he scored from a last minute free kick in the 2005 All-Ireland semi-final to secure a 1–13 to 1–12 victory over Armagh

The GAA's reasons for amateurism, apart from the fact that the financial sums just don't add up if we were to go pay for play, is that it ties in with the cultural aspect. It epitomises the selfless dedication of the player who wants only one thing; success with his teammates, all of whom are neighbours of his and share the same dreams and world view that he has.

Jarlath Burns
(Armagh footballer 1988–2001)

The players who really count on a team are those who do things when it really matters; they make a great tackle, or have the balls to go and get a score when it is badly needed, or dive in on a ball on the ground when the boots are flying. That is what leadership is all about.

Colm O'Rourke
(Meath footballer 1975–1995)

You are lucky to be born in a county like Cork. It's a big county with a great hurling tradition. There's a great sense of pride in being picked to play for Cork at any level. But in particular, a senior hurler and a senior All-Ireland medal holder in Cork is accorded a certain respect and status.

Jimmy Barry-Murphy
(Cork hurler and footballer 1973–1986, Cork hurling manager 1996–2001, 2011–)

I realised at WIT [Waterford Institute of Technology] the effort that must be put in to achieve. I found out here the harder you train the better you get.

Henry Shefflin
(Kilkenny hurler 1998–)

While it is hard to be continually innovative in the modern GAA sporting arena, it is the endless need for achievement and perpetual struggle for success that excites and inspires leaders like Mickey Harte and Brian Cody to always find that 'edge' that makes the difference.

Peter Canavan
(Tyrone footballer 1989–2005)

There are too many counties around this country that don't buy in to what is required and what is necessary to play an elite level of sport. There's no big secret to success or being successful. It's hard work, it's honesty, it's pride in what you are doing, it's teamwork.

Tommy Carr
(Dublin footballer 1985–1993)

The weaker counties may in a sense be lost sheep, but we must always keep looking out for them, because I feel very strongly that the right to play hurling is a cultural thing that must be respected.

George O'Connor
(Wexford hurler 1979–1996)

The most skilful player in the world won't necessarily win a game for you. The guy who's gonna do the business for you is the one who takes responsibility. He's not going to hide, not going to just mind his own position. Winning or losing games comes down to people being prepared to be unselfish.

Nicky English
(Tipperary hurler 1982–1996, Tipperary hurling manager 1999–2002)

There can't be a better feeling in the world for a Dublin player than seeing Hill 16 alive with blue flags when things are going well in a big championship game.

Barney Rock
(Dublin footballer 1980–1991)

The mentality [Jim] McGuinness [2012 All-Ireland winning Donegal manager] has imbued in his players starts with work ethic and ends with trust. It means if corner back Frank McGlynn sprints eighty metres up the field he can catch his breath while another man covers the vacant station. That's what makes them so formidable; any player can attack from anywhere, knowing he will be covered.

John O'Keefe
(Kerry footballer – writing in The Irish Times *in 2012)*

Loughnane was a brute. He was ruthless, a rough man on the training field. But he always did it with the aim of improving the team.

Brian Lohan
(Clare hurler 1992–2006)

on Ger Loughnane's training regime with Clare in the 1990s

When somebody tells you all your life that something is beyond your reach, that it's impossible, that you'll never get there, and then you do, well – there's that feeling that the work and toil that you put yourself through for thirteen or fourteen years has all come to fruition.

Kieran McGeeney
(Armagh footballer 1992–2007, Kildare manager, 2007–)

Everything we did was about putting on size and developing ourselves as footballers. Every morning we would get up and do 50 to 100 push-ups … We also regularly got up early before training, sometimes at 6 a.m., and went to the park with a handball target to practice our skills. We'd do hundreds of handballs each, then go back home, grab some breakfast and head to training.

Tadhg Kennelly
(Kerry footballer 2009 and Australian Rules footballer with the Sydney Swans 2001–2011)
on his training regime in Australia

The International Rules series was a bit like the Vietnam War. Nobody at home cared about it, but everyone involved sure did.

Leigh Matthews
(legendary Australian coach on the Australian players' passion for the International Rules series)

Our games were in a most grievous condition until the brave and patriotic men who started the Gaelic Athletic Association took their revival in hand. The Association's work has done more for Ireland than all the speeches of politicians for the past five years. Besides reviving our national sports, the GAA has also revived national memories, the names of its clubs perpetuating the memory of many great and good Irishmen.

Douglas Hyde
(founder of the Gaelic League in 1893, President of Ireland 1938–1945)

speaking in November 1892

You need split-second control, instant first touch. And you don't get those out of a book. You get them by practising.

Brian Cody
(Kilkenny hurling manager 1998–)

A mhunitir na Gaillimhe: tar éis seacht mbliain agus caoga, tá craobh na hÉireann ar ais i nGallaimh. Tá daoine ar ais i nGallaimh agus tá gliondar ina gcroí. Ach freisin caithfimid cuimhne ar daoine i Sasana i Mericea ar fud na tire agus tá said ag caoineadh anois láthair ...

(People of Galway: after fifty-seven years the All-Ireland is back in Galway. There are people back in Galway with wonder in their hearts. But also we must remember [Galway] people in England, in America and around the world maybe are crying at this moment ...)

People of Galway, we love you!

Joe Connolly
(Galway hurler 1976–1984)

in his captain's speech after the 1980 All-Ireland final win against Limerick

Defining what makes a great team is difficult. A team must be physically powerful, athletic, masters of the skills, be organised and they must have a killer instinct.

Michael 'Babs' Keating
(Tipperary hurler and footballer 1964–1975, Tipperary hurling manager 1987–1994, 2005–2007)

It's in your soul. It's spiritual. If football is in the pit of your belly then it's difficult to live without. Shapes your life, relegates the unimportant, distorts reality and drags you relentlessly in one direction.

Páidí Ó Sé
(Kerry footballer 1975–1987, Kerry football manager 1996–2003, Westmeath manager 2004–2006, Clare manager 2006)

The Mayo team were training one night, and a designated drill involved leaping in the air to catch an imaginary football. If anything, the exercise was ahead of standard thinking, designed to improve timing and focus, but the more traditional players were dubious about its usefulness. The squad of Mayomen moved across McHale Park under the floodlights, leaping every few yards for footballs that were not there. Near the halfway line, Anthony Finnerty suddenly broke away and began jogging towards the dressing room on his own. The manager shouted after him, demanding to know where he thought he was heading. 'I'm goin' to get me gloves,' Finnerty called back. 'The ball is wet.'

Keith Duggan
(journalist)

describing alternative training methods employed in the mid 1990s, in his book on Mayo football House of Pain *(2007)*

The biggest thing was the emphasis on skills development. Every session started with basic skills work. You might kick a ball back and across with another player maybe fifty times – left foot, right foot. You then work on the hand pass – right hand, left hand. They never allowed you to lose contact with the basic skills. As a coach now I put more emphasis on the skills side.

Paul Earley
(Roscommon footballer 1982–1994, and Australian Rules footballer with Melbourne Football Club 1984)

on his Australian Rules training experience

The only time in my playing days I heard anybody talking about hamstrings was when they were hanging outside a butcher's shop.

Mickey 'Rattler' Byrne
(Tipperary hurler 1949–1959)

Frank Cummins, one of our midfielders in the 1982 All-Ireland final, worked in demolition. He was knocking a wall with a sledgehammer down in Cork until five to twelve the night before the final and only got the train up to Dublin the morning of the match. I doubt you would see that nowadays.

Joe Hennessy
(Kilkenny hurler 1976–1988)

If I didn't believe, I wouldn't be here – it's as simple as that. You know it's not easy to be an inter-county footballer from any county. We train so much and so hard. If you don't believe that you can get to an All-Ireland final or you don't believe that you can get to an All-Ireland final and win it, then there's no point in playing.

Barry Moran
(Mayo footballer 2005–)

I felt that if you were playing in the full forward line and you get possession, your first option has to be to go for goal yourself, turn, beat your man and go for it.

Noel Lane
(Galway hurler 1977–1990, Galway hurling manager 2000–2002)

Watching a game on the wireless was torture: a great many members of my generation would have died long ago of cardiac failure but for their salutary diet of tea and bread-and-butter and black pudding and bacon and spuds and cabbage. And Micheál O'Hehir, God love him, would have been responsible: we had to listen, torn by apprehension as opponents carried the ball towards the goal: 'He's gone 10 yards. He's gone 20 yards. He's gone 30 yards. He's gone 40 yards. Oh, dear God, stop him in his tracks.'

Con Houlihan
(sports journalist)

Playing hurling for the parish gave us a great sense of pride and it became for the parish a uniting force. It was and is a strong force behind any country parish. It was and is a medium that makes conversation easy and the whole social fabric of the parish is enhanced. It gives the parish a focal point of which they can be proud.

Fr Iggy Clarke
(Galway hurler 1972–1984)

If I had to condense my life in hurling into one sentence and to say what I most achieved from the game I would have to say the friends I made and also the fact that it is the greatest way of all to start a conversation.

Liam Fennelly
(Kilkenny hurler 1981–1992)

The more football you play, the more you realise the only way of getting a bit of team spirit and morale going is to train your backside off with each other.

Oisín McConville
(Armagh footballer 1994–2008)

Gaelic Park at that time was fantastic, even if the pitch was a little dilapidated. On any given Sunday there would be five or six hurling or football matches and there was a congregation of Irish people in the afternoon and you would have had eight or ten or twelve thousand people there ... it was phenomenal in America at that time.

Larry Tompkins
(Kildare footballer 1979–1985 and Cork footballer 1987–1996)

on the thrill of playing in front of the diehard GAA Diaspora in New York in the 1980s

It's like anything, like a new job, you have to work hard and prove yourself to the new manager because they are obviously going to have their own views.

Paul Flynn
(Dublin footballer 2008–)

on trying to prove himself under the new Dublin manager, Jim Galvin

I would have marked Sheehy or Spillane any day before Egan. We often recall his point in the 1977 semi-final. As he came through I shadowed him, waiting for the moment to use my shoulder. When I hit him I made perfect contact. He had to go down. He did, but he just bounced back up in the same movement, feinted left, moved to the right and put over an exceptional point. What could anybody have done?

Gay O'Driscoll
(Dublin footballer 1965–1979)

on the Kerry great, John Egan

It was always my dream to play in Croke Park. When I was growing up going up to Croke Park looking at Dublin and Kerry, I used to sit there thinking, yeah, I'd love to be out there.

Francie Bellew
(Armagh footballer 2002–2009)

You had all this energy and hype and the movement on the field and the hits and the referee's decisions and the scores, and then it all comes down to those last two minutes [of an All-Ireland final] when the whole thing is decided but it is not quite over. That gap, I suppose, is where I always dreamed of being. And standing there was amazing.

John O'Mahony
(Leitrim football manager 1992–1996, Mayo football manager 1987–1991, 2006–2010, Galway football manager 1997–2004)

Don't for one minute think that we were going to get bored with it. Winning All-Irelands! I was born in a place called Sneem. Any fella who had any ambition, it was to play for Kerry. There was no soccer, no hurling, no nothing. And to play for Kerry was the dream. I got on a successful Kerry team that won All-Irelands. Why should a fella get off it? The power and the glory!

John Egan
(Kerry footballer 1975–1984)

Hurling has always been a way of life with me. It was never my ambition to play the game for the sake of winning All-Ireland medals or breaking records, but to perfect the art as well as possible.

Christy Ring
(Cork hurler 1939–1963)

If he hits the ball like he did in the first half, this will end up in Clonliffe College. Yes, it's gone over Hill 16 and out over the railway. That sliotar will play no more hurling today.

Micheál Ó Muircheartaigh
(legendary GAA commentator)

There is no getting away from it, if you want to do well, it takes a lot of time. It's not just about the training. It's about the preparation that goes into your training and your interaction with individuals within the team. The players have lives to live as well. You have to try and accommodate them any way you can. It takes time to think about that and explore things with players. It's not just a football business, it's a people business.

Mickey Harte
(Tyrone football manager 2003–)

When you play in a packed Croke Park, you can hear nothing, not even your teammates calling for the ball, so you just have to go wholeheartedly for everything. There's so much noise that some things become peripheral. To be honest, I didn't even notice that it was raining until it was mentioned after the game.

Gregory McCartan
(Down footballer 1990–2003)

Looking back on my hurling career I find that it helped me in a great way in developing my character. The greatest memory I have is the friendship I made with the players I played with and the players I played against. Today we can look back and enjoy our moments of glory.

John Fenton
(Cork hurler 1975–1987)

My philosophy of life is living to the full while we're here and to exercise. I walk a solid hour every single day, you don't have to be running or jogging. I don't go overboard on diets or anything – that's crazy – good walking is the best of all.

Mick O'Dwyer
(Kerry footballer 1956–1974, Kerry football manager 1974–1989, Kildare manager 1991–1994, 1997–2002, Laois manager 2002–2006, Wicklow manager 2006–2011, Clare manager 2013–)

You just have to go in with no fear and not be worried about your body taking a beating. You have to go in and flake hard at your own peril. You have to keep going and you have to be relentless.

Darragh Ó Sé
(Kerry footballer 1993–2010)

The warmth of those people was incredible. It kind of dawned on me then. The whole thing hit me and in my heart and soul I shed a tear or two inside. That is what I had been doing this thing for – thirteen years of breaking arms, legs, nose, jaw, the hundreds of training sessions, the whole lot – that is why. These were strangers standing in the pissing rain to greet a team that had been destroyed in the biggest football match of the year. I won't ever forget that.

David Brady
(Mayo footballer 1996–2008)

paying tribute to the hundreds of Mayo supporters who waited in heavy rain to welcome home their countymen who had just lost the 2006 All-Ireland final by a record margin to Kerry

As a player you want to get into your routine pre championship games, you get into your own bubble and really other people's opinions don't really matter to you. You have to be mentally strong in the build-up to these big games.

Brendan Cummins
(Tipperary hurling goalkeeper 1995–)

Henry, a man frequently more dangerous when he didn't have the ball than when he did, not interested by the compulsion or the misplaced ego to insist on doing everything by himself, grandmastering matters from wherever he chose to take up station. A fifteen-man game, and he didn't forget it. It was only by a quirk of spelling that there is an I in Shefflin.

Enda McEvoy
on Henry Shefflin, in his book The Godfather of Modern Hurling: The Father Tommy Maher Story *(2012)*

I'm not too sure what other hurlers do, but I know that there was many an 'Our Father' said during the parade [on All-Ireland final day]. Obviously you're deep in thought, deep in concentration but you're also asking for any divine help you can get at that stage!

Adrian Ronan
(Kilkenny hurler 1989–1999)

The night before I'd have three or four grand pints in the local pub, the safest place to be. And on match day you'd go into the dressing room, the lads'd be banging the hurl off the table, they'd be psyching. I'd go in, tap the ball off the shower wall, get togged out and then go in and just have the last fag.

Johnny Pilkington
(Offaly hurler 1988–2001)

on his preparations for a big match in Croke Park

My success as a player was due to a combination of factors: inner drive, belief, hard work and commitment. I was not blessed with natural talent, but I was a slogger and I made sacrifices, worked hard and I was selfish. I was also focused and single-minded. You have to be to make it to the top.

Pat Spillane
(Kerry footballer 1975–1991, now a GAA analyst)

After all the fuss, the money and the hype, you remember the friends, the contacts, the games and the amount it [the GAA] means to people everywhere in the country. If I were ever to go away from home, I know I'd look back and think that that is what being Irish is all about. That's home.

Jason Sherlock
(Dublin footballer 1995–2010)

Perception is everything when you are a manager. You have to appear to the world at large to be a very co-operative person, always willing to talk to the media and sounding so sincere that everybody who reads your words will believe them. You can remain popular, always be believed and yet never say anything that gives away any of the real secrets of how you carry out your football business.

Eugene Magee
(All-Ireland winning football manager with Offaly in 1982, GAA analyst and chair of the Football Review Committee 2012)

We were never told to hurl, we were never told to get outside and play hurling. You know, it was just something that came naturally to us, it's just our culture, a way of life.

Ollie Canning
(Galway hurler 1996–2010)

Going away is part of an army career. There was this immense sense of sadness about the prospect of missing football. The army had a system at the time of informing all those abroad of events at home by means of a newsletter which always gave the GAA results. I would receive a result and be able to picture the ground the game was played at and the colours of the teams. I passed a lot of hours imagining games at home, many Sundays wondering how Roscommon were getting on.

Dermot Earley Snr
(Roscommon footballer 1965–1985 and Chief of Staff of the Irish Army 2007–2010)

Teaspean an t-oilteacht dom agus imróig mé níos fearr.

(Show me the skill and I will play better)

Proverb

After much consideration I have come to the conclusion that the GAA is really all about Bill Doonan heading for Monte Casino. Bill was a member of a family of travellers that settled in Cavan and he was a natural footballer. He was also a wayward Paddy and having joined the Army, and been trained as a radio operator, he itched for action in the real war that raged in Europe and elsewhere at the time. Bill deserted, crossed the Border and joined the British Army.

In the autumn of 1943 the war in southern Italy raged and Bill Doonan was radio operator with his unit. One Sunday afternoon in September he was no longer to be seen. He vanished as if the ground had swallowed him. It was considered unlikely that he had been shot as there was a lull in the hostilities at the time. It was a mystery.

A search was mounted and they found him at last. Even when they did they found it difficult to attract his attention. He was up a tree on the side of a steep hill and seemed to be in a trance. And in a way he was, for after much effort and experimentation, Private Doonan had eventually homed in on the commentary of the second half of the All-Ireland football final between Roscommon and Cavan from Croke Park.

He was too indispensable to be court-marshalled and survived the war to play soccer for a year with Lincoln City and afterwards win two All-Irelands with Cavan; one in the Polo Grounds, New York in 1947 and another in Croke Park the following year.

If anyone ever asks you what the GAA is all about just think of Bill Doonan, the wanderer, on the side of that hill, in the middle of a World War … at home.

Breandán Ó hEithir
(journalist and author)

from the last page of his book Over the Bar *(1984)*

The mental attitude of the athlete in training is of paramount importance if full benefit is to be derived. Freedom from personal anxieties or worries is an essential condition for training. Training must be undertaken always in a spirit of lightheartedness and freedom from worry and ennui, which will automatically pave the way for the development of full psycho-physical fitness.

Dr Éamon O'Sullivan
from his seminal coaching book The Art and Science of Gaelic Football *(1958)*

That has been the basic cornerstone that has supported every team I have ever produced. They work. They don't flinch. They hound and hustle and harry. They tackle. They win the ball back. Then, they create.

Mickey Harte
(Tyrone football manager 2003–)

Then there was the turn round Barry's corner. You're looking down Patrick Street at thousands of people. It was just a red sea all the way. Forget about Moses looking down on the Holy Land – the view from the All-Ireland winning lorry as you round Barry's Corner is the greatest sight a Corkman could ever see.

Billy Morgan
(Cork hurler and footballer 1966–1981 and Cork football manager 1986–1996, 2003–2007)

Football is to Kerry what films are to Hollywood: a county-wide obsession that sets a pecking order, discussed endlessly and by everyone, complete with its own arcane laws and rituals. Football talk is no idle form of gossip here, but a crucial element in the county's psyche, to which business, love, the land and the weather regularly take second place.

Pat Spillane
(Kerry footballer 1975–1991 and GAA analyst)

I play football for enjoyment and success – to win All-Irelands. There's an inner pride thing that motivates you. In Kerry you should be competing and competitive to win All-Irelands every year.

Colm 'Gooch' Cooper
(Kerry footballer 2002–)

What was also enlightening about last Sunday's All-Ireland [Donegal v Mayo 2012] was being able to sit back and enjoy the game of Gaelic football for what it is – an honest sport where men give and take the hard knocks and get on with it.

Shay Given
(soccer goalkeeper for Blackburn 1994–1997, Newcastle 1997–2009, Manchester City 2009–2011, Aston Villa 2011 and Ireland 1996–2012)

It says an awful lot about this team. There was an awful lot said about them, but they showed great courage and conviction over the years and now they've got their reward. I do hope other counties, the likes of Down, will take heart and know that failure is only fuel for success. It's a great day to be a Rebel!

Conor Counihan
(Cork footballer 1981–1993, Cork football manager 2008–)

after his team won the All-Ireland in 2010 following many attempts

There is no magic formula for managing a team. It is largely a matter of being in the right place at the right time and creating the right environment for success.

Seán Boylan
(Meath manager 1983–2006)

Some people think it all falls out of the sky – it [the development of a GAA community abroad] happens because of dedication and often lonely work by those who keep going when all of the circumstances seem against them. The migrant experience is a special experience. We can see the legacy that the generations have handed on and how their Irishness was important to them. In choosing to accentuate their Irishness they weren't denying the essence of culture to anyone else.

Michael D. Higgins
(President of Ireland 2011–)

speaking at the Ruislip GAA grounds in London, where he became the first Irish head of state to visit a GAA facility in Britain

I was waiting under a dropping ball with Phil Stuart of Derry when I caught a glimpse of a pair of knees above my shoulder and hands gripping the ball. It was Mick O'Connell.

Seamus Murphy
(Kerry footballer 1958–1970)

on his long-time midfield partner

If new management is in place then this initial meeting is of even greater importance. From the moment the new man walks into the room many sets of eyes will be locked on him. His mannerisms and initial words will create an impression, one way or the other. How he is received at this first gathering could go a long way in determining what route the months ahead will take.

Peter Canavan
(Tyrone footballer 1989–2005)

It was not long until we knew we were in Mayo. Along the line were cocks of hay that were saturated in paraffin. As the train sped by, the hay was set ablaze and proud farmers and supporters held their beacons aloft as the train sped on into the night. At Ballyhaunis, fog signals exploded and as the train came to a halt eager and frenzied supporters ran down the platform with blazing torches and hoisted the cup aloft.

John Healy
(journalist)

from the article 'The March Triumphal' in Western People, September 1950

I love the company of GAA people. I love it. Anytime, anywhere, give me a GAA person to talk to and we'll get on. GAA people are the heart of what this country is all about.

Tommy Lyons
(Offaly football manager 1997–1999, Dublin football manager 2002–2004)

I played hurling with Waterford when I was younger. I played all the way up to minors and then went across to play the other [soccer]. Going back to hurling was the plan. If I'm capable of playing at that level I would love to do it again when I retire. I was on a par with players that went on to do great things so you wouldn't know what might happen in the future.

Stephen Hunt
(soccer player for Wolves 2010– and Ireland 2007–)

It's a life-changing moment for a player. You are no longer Michael Murphy. You are Michael Murphy the All-Ireland winner and that is a great title to have and no one can take that away from them. That's the enjoyment I get out of it.

Jim McGuinness
(Donegal football manager 2010–)

The island clay felt good beneath his feet
A man undeceived by victory or defeat.

Brendan Kennelly
(poet and Kerryman)

*on the twenty-two-year-old Mick O'Connell who
captained Kerry to All-Ireland victory in 1959 and
left Croke Park without the cup, returning to Valentia
Island later that night, rowing home in the darkness*

Be fair, be balanced in your approach to things,
don't hit anyone unfairly and walk off the pitch
with the respect of your opponents. The man
that's a thug on the field is a thug off it, you can
never trust him. Character stands out a mile,
on and off the field, quality stands out like a
beacon.

Séamus Durack
(Clare hurling goalkeeper 1969–83)

For me, there are special moments on the field. I think they are the moments for which I play, especially when the final whistle sounds and you've won, and for a split second you experience a sense of peace, a great self-satisfaction. That moment is total contentment, and how many times in our lives do any of us feel 100% content?

Liam Hayes
(Meath footballer 1983–1996)

in his autobiography Out of Our Skins *(1992)*

I know players definitely want to see their manager active on the sideline. It makes them feel that someone really cares about what is happening on the field.

Dickie Murphy
(well-known inter-county hurling referee)

When the final whistle ended the game, and I realised we were All-Ireland champions, I was totally elated. I thought of my dream as a child playing in the back garden and how it had actually come true. It was a lovely, very satisfying feeling.

Trevor Giles
(Meath footballer 1994–2005)

Our conviction is that 'The Killarney Experience' is a cameo of the heart-and-soul of the GAA. That heart-and-soul thrives across Ireland – and, of course, Tyrone – on a daily basis. To tap into it and to help sustain it, just get involved, at whatever level, in whatever place.

Long after the thousands had left Fitzgerald Stadium last Saturday evening our Tyrone team was getting ready for a bitter journey home. Around 500 Kerry people remained outside the changing area – men and women, old and young. As our people started to board their coach a ripple of applause met them. That ripple grew and grew and for long minute after long minute just went on and on and on.

When Mickey Harte appeared, a cheer of support went up. As the coach headed down through Killarney hundreds on the pavements took over where the others left off, warmly applauding Tyrone. There is no doubt that Ireland lost a lot and took a lot of wrong turns in the last few years. But if you wanted your faith in decency, respect, honour and dignity restored, then Killarney at about eight o'clock last Saturday evening was the place to be.

Inspirational. Unforgettable. Classy.

Post on the Tyrone GAA website in July 2012 in response to the applause given to the Tyrone team after their championship match against Kerry in Killarney

To me, that was living. People are very rarely 'alive', you know. And for those twenty minutes in extra time what was going through my mind was: 'This is unbelievable. Because those boys are in the thick of this now. Every moment counts and they are living on the edge. And it would be brilliant if they can come through this and win but even if they don't, this is going to be a great life experience.' Because in that moment they were living in the fullest sense. The atmosphere that evening was as raw as I have ever felt. And the lights coming on made it too. It was all kind of magical.

Jim McGuinness
(Donegal football manager 2010–)

on the Donegal v Kildare match in 2011 that got them through to the semi-final of the All-Ireland

The ship has sprung a leak but we are not going down!

Ger Loughnane
(Clare hurler 1973–1987, Clare hurling manager 1994–2000, Galway manager 2006–2008)

speaking to his team at half time in the 1995 Munster final when Clare were trailing by four points – they went on to win the game

I've always been a huge supporter of this game and whenever you do get a chance to pull on that jersey and play with the best players in Ireland it is something special.

Seán Cavanagh
(Tyrone footballer 2002–)

on the International Rules series

There was an uncle of mine and that was always his advice to me – don't give away frees! Let them hit it and they might hit it wide, but if they have any kind of free-taker at all, all you're doing is giving away an easy point. I always agreed with that as a player and it's something I carried into management, I keep saying to the lads. I always counted a free given away and scored as a point conceded, while some eejits don't see it like that at all. They prefer to give away a point from a free, when they should be just trying to defend, maybe put a fella off his shot.

Anthony Daly
(Clare hurler 1989–2000, Clare hurling manager 2003–2006, Dublin hurling manager 2008–)

I love to see a player banging a ball off a wall then controlling it. I could make the ball talk. I could bend it, put top-spin on it, anything I wanted. That was from training on my own. I'd finish school in the evening, go home, throw my schoolbag into the corner and get my hurley and ball, and the dog, and we'd come up to Semple Stadium, hurl 'til 6 o'clock in the evening. I'd go home and have my supper, get the hurley and ball again and back up, stay at it 'til dark, 10 or 11 o'clock at night.

Jimmy Doyle
(Tipperary hurler 1957–1973)

The difference between winning a club and a county All-Ireland is, when you get a slap on the back after the match, you actually know the person when you turn around.

Tomás Meehan
(Galway footballer 1998–2007)

When forwards decide to do an extra bit of work by themselves and go to the pitch for shooting practice, one thing they often try to do is score from the angles in which their scoring ratio isn't great. But all shooting practice should be done from in front of the posts around the D area. The more times you kick points from there, the more confidence you will gain to do it from other areas of the pitch. It is that simple.

Steven McDonnell
(Armagh footballer 1999–2012)

There has been a lot of talk about the work we did on the Hill of Tara – how fellows vomited their guts out, nearly died and so on. It had nothing to do with playing football, but had everything to do with stamina, with fellows finding inner strength – because the first thing to go under pressure is the gut.

Seán Boylan
(Meath football manager 1983–2006)

With them b*****ds of mountains in front of us, and those hoors of lakes behind us, sure there's nothing to do but play football.

Jackie Lyne
(Kerry footballer 1944–1954)

Gaelic games exist in bizarre places and sometimes with no Irish involvement whatsoever. At a recent tournament in Budapest, the Viking Gaels boasted a team made up solely of Scandinavian girls, many of whom had never been to Ireland. In the Brittany region of France there is an enormous interest in Celtic heritage and culture, and it is not unusual to find teams that don't have a single English-speaking player, let alone an Irish person in their ranks.

Philip O'Connor
(author)

in his book A Parish Far From Home *(2011)*

Above all, great managers radiate certainty where none exists. They refuse to admit to a scintilla of self-doubt because good management is as much the creation of illusion as the construction of a co-operative.

Vincent Hogan
(journalist)

Is fada an turas é ó Fhidsí go Corcaigh agus ó Chorcaigh go Páirc an Chrócaigh!

(It's a long journey from Fiji to Cork and from Cork to Croke Park!)

Seán Óg Ó hAilpín
(Cork hurler 1995–2012)

from the opening lines of his captain's speech after he led Cork to All-Ireland victory in 2005 – the speech was delivered entirely in Irish and is widely regarded as one of the best captain's speeches in GAA history

The stuff he did on field was unbelievable and really, for myself, I wouldn't be here if it wasn't for Jimmy Stynes, because he was the trailblazer, he was the one that set the tone for people with different backgrounds. I'm indebted to the man because I wouldn't be standing here today. I would not have played one game of AFL football if it wasn't for Jim Stynes. He was the first bloke with a different background, different culture to come out and play it successfully. I was in awe of him. I would be constantly on the phone to him. I would ask him for advice on a contract negotiation, stuff like that. Jim's legacy is going to be enormous.

Tadhg Kennelly
(Kerry footballer 2009 and Australian Rules footballer with the Sydney Swans 2001–2011)

This is Hampstead Heath in London. Two or three hundred of the old boys used to come up here on a Sunday religiously. Sometimes they would bring a couple of clothes hangers with them and extend the aerial using the clothes hangers to give them better sound.

from the RTÉ Radio documentary, Sex, Flights and Videotapes, *describing fanatical Irish GAA fans in London in the early 1960s gathering on London's highest point, Hampstead Heath, to tune in to RTÉ Radio on a championship Sunday*

You can't hide, even if you're scoring well you must keep working, and if things aren't working out for you, you concentrate on stopping your own man from hurling anyway, from doing any damage. Don't rest on your laurels if you're getting a few scores, but don't give up either if things aren't going right for you.

Henry Shefflin
(Kilkenny hurler 1998–)

Getting in their heads. That's what the game is about. It's an extremely important part to be sure. Get them on the right wavelength. What we went through together was deeper than just football. We'd be concerned about each other – concerned about anything which would perturb a player.

Kevin Heffernan
(Dublin footballer 1948–1962, Dublin football manager 1973–1976 and 1979–1983)

Have the hurley in your hand for up to twenty minutes every day of the week, and practise your striking, your ball control. Even ten minutes a day is better than a two-hour session once a week. I would always have a hurley and a ball; even if I was only sent to the shop I'd bring the hurley and ball.

John Fenton
(Cork hurler 1975–1987)

Parents are always going to have a huge influence on your life. We were always brought to training and matches and were kicking in the back garden. They started us off basically.

Tomás Ó Sé
(Kerry footballer 2000–)

I'm doing a lot of flexibility, yoga, swimming and staying out of contact in training as much as I can, which is probably something that I didn't pay much attention to when I was younger. I think four or five years of heavy training and contact takes its toll, so it's more or less trying to watch yourself more than anything.

Trevor Mortimer
(Mayo footballer 2000–2012)
on alternative training methods that helped extend his inter-county career

One exercise they use much is hurling. They strike a ball with a stick they call a comaan [*sic*], about three and a half feet long. They seldom come off without broken heads or shins, in which they glory.

John Duddon
(an English visitor to Kildare in 1699)

Play with both feet – the likes of Colm Cooper can play the ball with left or right. If you are comfortable off either foot, it will get you a long way.

Alan Brogan
(Dublin footballer 2002–)
with advice for young players

I call for the Irish people to take the management of their games into their own hands, to encourage and promote every form of athletics which is peculiarly Irish.

Michael Cusack
(founder of the GAA)

We are within thirty seconds of the end of the most incredible series of football matches that were ever played in any code the world over, ever. We have two seconds of added time after the most incredible finale in any sport. Is what we have just seen real?

Micheál Ó Muircheartaigh
(legendary GAA commentator)

commentating on the last moments of the fourth game between Meath and Dublin in the scorching summer of 1991, a four-match saga which gripped the entire country

In Kerry we make up for our remoteness from the world with our ability at football. It's a cliché, but it's part of the identity of the county and its people, part of the way we express ourselves and project an image of Kerry for others and ourselves. We win and we win with style.

Jack O'Connor
(Kerry football manager 2003–2006 and
2008–2012)

If you can play well for five minutes, then, with practice, you can play well for eight minutes, and gradually progress. It is a question of getting the body physically ready and then developing the mentality to be able to concentrate for a particular length of time.

Seán Boylan
(Meath football manager 1983–2006)

I'd managed to keep everything under control for the warm-up and the first half, but I lost it as soon as I heard the words, 'Tadhg, you're going on.' I stood up, took off my tracksuit top and then waited in the intersection box. Immediately I started to well up. It was all I'd ever wanted to do: wear a senior jersey in a game.

Tadhg Kennelly
(Kerry footballer 2009 and Australian Rules footballer with the Sydney Swans 2001–2011)

on playing his first senior game for Kerry in 2009, from his book Unfinished Business *(2009)*

Meath are like Dracula. They're never dead till there's a stake through their heart.

Martin Carney
(Donegal footballer 1970–1979, Mayo footballer 1979–1990 and GAA analyst)

I have a very simple philosophy. You work extremely hard, do everything to prepare the team. Try to educate them in relation to what you want to achieve and trust them to go do it.

Jim McGuinness
(Donegal football manager 2010–)

Develop your hurling on your own. Always have the hurley in your hand, become so used to it that it's just an extension of your arm. The most important drill you'll ever do in hurling is the ball off the wall, back and forward, first touch, and the beauty of it is that you can do it by yourself, on your own.

Liam Griffin
(Wexford hurling manager 1995–1996)

If you passed the ball to Keher, or he stood over a free, all you had to do was run back out to your position for the puck-out.

Mick Crotty
(Kilkenny hurler 1969–1980)

on his teammate Eddie Keher, the highest scorer in Ireland 1966–1972

I've always had a soft spot for the Irish, but ever since last Sunday I've been annoyed by them. Annoyed with them for keeping this great game of hurling to themselves for so long. I've seen sporting events in many parts of Europe and America (both North and South) but I have yet to see a game which keeps the excitement at such a constant fever pitch as hurling.

Kenneth Wolstenholme
(English sports commentator famous for his 'they think it's all over' commentary of the 1966 soccer World Cup)

There's a good edge to it over the last weeks. In every training session there'd be some minor incident that can spill over, and if that doesn't happen, it's been a poor training session! If there's not a minor thing between one or two players, you're thinking we're not going well. You want to replicate the championship intensity so you need that edge to happen.

Graham Canty
(Cork footballer 2001–)

If I had carte blanche on youngsters starting off in hurling, nine or ten years of age, I'd advise them to do four things: skip, ballet, Irish dancing and handball. Get your footwork right and you'll be a much better hurler.

D. J. Carey
(Kilkenny hurler 1988–2007)

We had a team meeting a few nights earlier. Boys had agreed that training had gone slack. Mick Lyons said we'd gone too soft. So this night we were training and I sidestepped Mick when he gave me this feckin' awful dirty belt. We exchanged words and I said to myself, 'If that happens again, I'm going to pull.' Anyway Mick did it again and I turned around and hit him as hard as I could. Next thing, all I could see was blood. I split his nose down the middle. I spent the rest of that training session looking around, left, right and centre. I genuinely had a fear that I was going to wake up in hospital. I kept out of Mick's way for the rest of the training session. He never said a word, just let the blood flow down his nose. But I remember going into the dressing room after and there was hardly a word spoken. I was thinking to myself, 'You're fighting for your life here.' I went into the showers and it was like something from *Midnight Express* with the steam rising and everything. I reversed in and positioned myself so that if anyone came in, I could see them. Next thing, Mick walks in, and I swear to God, I clenched my fist down by my side and said to myself, 'If he pulls, I'll pull first.' What does Mick Lyons do? He lifts his arm but instead of hitting me he puts it around me. 'That's the sort of stuff we f****n' need!' After me splitting him! I said, 'Mick, I didn't mean to split you but it's just you hit me ...' He said, 'Don't worry about it. It's only blood.' With that I unclenched my fist, finished my shower and when I walked out, I looked back over my shoulder and all I could see was Mick showering away, blood and shampoo mixing together. That was Mick Lyons. The best captain I ever played under. That was Meath. That was football back in those days.

Bernard Flynn
(Meath footballer 1984–1994)

on training in the lead-up to the four-game saga against the Dubs in 1991

Mental preparation on its own is a waste of time. That's why I wouldn't call myself a sports psychologist. Because, if your physical conditioning is not good, if your lifestyle isn't good, if your technical coaching hasn't been good, if your tactical awareness isn't good, you're just not going to win.

Enda McNulty
(Armagh footballer 1996–2010)

I always reckoned you'd know what line not to cross with a referee. He has a very hard job to do on such a big pitch. I never argued with a referee because there's no point. They're not going to change their mind. Have you ever seen a decision changed because a player argued with a referee? And if you accept his decision you might get a break later on.

Mick Lyons
(Meath footballer 1979–1992)

The defender's job is always to try and look after your own man. My job was just to try to keep my man from scoring, then try and get on the ball myself and hit balls up to the forwards. That's all you're thinking of in the game. There're always different things, but the main thing is you have to think for yourself on the field. You just have to go out and prepare for whatever happens and you have to be able to think on your feet.

Tommy Walsh
(Kilkenny hurler 2002–)

In the end what happens on the field is a reflection of many many things, most of which we can't see from the sideline.

Eamon Dunphy
(soccer player with Millwall 1965–1975 and Ireland 1965–1971 and analyst)

The thing about it is, in football you see it even in local games at home, teams winning games they should never win. It's all about attitude and preparation, and if the attitude is right you will go a long way. No matter how bad a team you are, you know that if your attitude is right then you know that you are in with a fighting chance. If the attitude isn't right, no matter how good you are, it's hard to turn it around. Attitude is everything and it's all about getting it right on the day, regardless of the team you are playing against.

Brian Sheehan
(Kerry footballer 2000–)

That was hard to swallow, being beaten in the Munster final by eighteen points. But, you know, if you go through enough of those days and keep coming back for more, you'll eventually come good, and we did.

Anthony Daly
(Clare hurler 1989–2000, Clare hurling manager 2003–2006, Dublin hurling manager 2008–)

'Go out there and give them plenty of timber. Drive 'em into the ground. Cut the heads off 'em. I want to see blood spilt.' Then just before we went out on the pitch the trainer blessed himself. 'Now lads, we'll all say a prayer that no one will be hurt.'

Billy Morgan
(Cork hurler, footballer 1966–1981 and Cork football manager 1986–1996, 2003–2007)

recalls a typical pre-match team talk in the dressing rooms of New York in the early 1980s

If you can let go of that fear in life then you can do anything. It allows you to really let go and chase the things you really want to do in your life and live out the life you were born to live.

Jim Stynes
(Dublin minor footballer 1983–1984 and Australian Rules footballer with Melbourne Football Club 1987–1998)

When I was younger I was told that there were two marks a Kerryman puts in his diary, Munster final day and All-Ireland final day. That's what we're faced with in this county. That's the measure.

Páidí Ó Sé
(Kerry footballer 1975–1987, Kerry football manager 1996–2003, Westmeath manager 2004–2006, Clare manager 2006)

They enjoy it. There's definitely too much made of it. I don't see articles being written about swimmers at twelve and thirteen years of age who get up at half-four every morning to train and then go to school. It sounds very exotic but it's a very practical thing and when they're out there they love it and then they're awake for the day and they're lively. I think the harshness of it, it isn't that bad. It's something they actually look forward to. We only do it around exam time and they really like to be up, particularly the students, to get their study in for the day. If we were doing five evenings a week they'd lose the evening and would get no work done, whereas in the early mornings they're in college by 8 a.m. and they're able to study. So there's a lifestyle thing that works for us.

Pat Gilroy
(Dublin football manager 2009–2012)

on the benefits of early morning training

If you cannot get motivated for a game against Dublin in Croke Park, live on television, in front of a big crowd, then you have no right to play county football. This is a day to get you motivated. It's the days you want to be involved in.

Paddy Keenan
(Louth footballer 2003–)

I've now won three All-Irelands with Tyrone, but I would still probably say that my proudest moment was standing in Melbourne in 2005 with the Irish squad, despite the fact that we were heavily beaten in both that game and the first Test. It was a source of immense pride to see all the tricolours around the stadium and hear 40,000 Irish singing the national anthem.

Seán Cavanagh
(Tyrone footballer 2002–)

Kilkenny hurlers? We'll see your four and raise you one.

Mary O'Connor
(Cork footballer 1996–2010)

in the captain's speech on the occasion of Cork's fifth ladies All-Ireland win in a row

I don't think it's sinking in just yet. You know probably afterwards when we reflect on it, it will probably sink in a bit more. At the moment it's a bit surreal, we can't believe that we've won the three in a row. It's such an historic thing to do.

Ursula Jacob
(Wexford camogie player 2004–)

after her side won the All-Ireland in 2012

We in the GAA are diminished as a community when players, whom we revere so much, display such an explicit sign of lost cultural self-confidence by disrespecting Amhrán na bhFiann. All over the world, you will see different groups of people giving expression to their vision of what it means to be Irish. Surely it is a fundamental element of that vision that one would stand to attention when one's national anthem is played at public events such as Gaelic football matches? Surely it behoves our county footballers, who represent a tradition and a heritage so cherished and so hard earned, to exercise autonomously all the faculties of a full-grown human being within that tradition by respecting the anthem? Surely that's not too much to ask for ... Is it?

Dara Ó Cinnéide
(Kerry footballer 1991–2007)

My name is Dermot A. Molloy. My hope for the future is to play for Donegal under 14, 16, minor then senior and to get an All-Ireland medal.

Dermot 'Brick' Molloy
(Donegal footballer 2007–)

opening paragraph of a homework assignment titled
'My Hopes for the Future', written when he was ten
years old

I played county football to win and that's all I did. I just loved winning. It drove me too far sometimes. I tried it many times before, not getting myself up, not getting myself ready for it. It just didn't work. I knew myself that I always play better when I am on the edge. At the end of the day I was getting no thanks when we were getting beat and I didn't have that game-face on.

Ryan McMenamin
(Tyrone footballer 1999–2012)

When I have American actors over I show them hurling games and they think we're wild, but the actual skill involved, conveying to them how few people get injured – we can forget how unique hurling is and how it makes us different to every other country in the world.

Fiach Mac Conghail
(artistic director of the Abbey Theatre 2011–)

I know it's a big sacrifice. You are spending a lot of time out of the house, but it's only over the last two years it's been the most enjoyable thing. Success has been enjoyable, but going to the gym, and every single training session, has been enjoyable. I think because you know you are getting something out of it. You know you are getting fitter, you know you are getting stronger. Of all the things I'd probably take a lot of satisfaction out of the training.

Colm McFadden
(Donegal footballer 2002–)

The Fermanagh players will not want to be treated as being substandard to the players in Tyrone. I will not be treating them as anything but equal. There are standards that you have to come to expect. In life, I certainly have not got anything easy. Anything I achieved was through hard work and graft. A lot of times you were fighting against the grain. That is something that I will be making clear to the players. Any success that you get, you have to earn it. You have to work very hard for it.

Peter Canavan
(Tyrone footballer 1989–2005 and Fermanagh manager 2011–)

on what he expected from the Fermanagh football team

Games grow out of the soil, just as plants do. Hurling grew out of the soil of Ireland.

Michael Cusack
(founder of the GAA)

I've always been involved in coaching, even when I was playing for the county. Over the years, my ideas have changed. I always try to evolve my methods, because you should never stop learning. I don't agree with trainers who think that fitness training and skills training should be mutually exclusive. I believe that all training should be done with the football. Through doing drills that involve the football, you do not only improve your fitness base, but also your skill level.

Liam Sammon
(Galway footballer 1966–1979 and Galway football manager 2007–2009)

Young people need to be inspired, told they can achieve anything they set their minds to.

Jim Stynes
(Dublin minor footballer 1983–1984 and Australian Rules footballer with Melbourne Football Club 1987–1998)

It's no longer about the emigrant going abroad and growing the GAA; it's about the emigrant gone abroad whose child is now playing games. That's where the growth is going to be.

Liam O'Neill
(GAA President 2012–)

Everyone in Ireland believes their own county to be the best. How did this happen? How did a system of convenience, imposed by the English rulers dating back to King John, come to hold such a firm grip on the Irish imagination? And yet people fiercely cling on to the idea that their county is God's own territory and champion its beauty spots and celebrate its patriots and famous sons in song and in statue.

Keith Duggan
(journalist)

I'd be optimistic. There's an awful lot of good hurlers. One of the things I have found is when we go to hurling counties – the level of coaching that's going on here, the standard of coaching we are doing is ahead of the other counties. People might think I'm joking when I say that, but when you go down to the Kilkennys, the Tipperarys, the Corks, the Limericks, they're not doing anything extra that we aren't. Our biggest problem is the lack of numbers.

Mick Scully
(Tipperary hurler 1985–1987, Laois underage hurling coach)

I really enjoy playing and training with both the club and county. We're lucky to have a very good club side there too. I've always loved it; the training has never bothered me; if you're not enjoying it, then it's time to give up.

Paul Barden
(Longford footballer 1998–)

Whether you're a professional or amateur sportsperson, the importance of diet cannot be stressed enough. People involved in sport have come to realise that you can't just eat anything if you want to perform to the best of your ability. Amateur sportspeople like GAA players have the hardest life because diet can be squeezed out owing to the fact that they're working a full-time job as well. Keeping well hydrated and joints flexible are also part of a good diet.

Jane Griffin
(sports dietician)

from her book Food for Sport: Eat Well, Perform Better *(2001)*

The simple premise is that you can probably address most things in life by one thing, and that's hard work.

Pat Gilroy
(Dublin football manager 2009–2012)

The hurling and football championships could boast an average attendance of 16,032 last year. You want to know how good this is for an amateur competition in a small country with a small population? It's better than the average for the Heineken Cup (14,423), the Brazilian Serie A soccer league (14,058), the Russian Premier soccer league (13,066) and England's Aviva Rugby Union Premiership (12,925). And it compares pretty well with the averages for America's mighty NHL (17,455) and NBA (17,244). If you're getting the sort of numbers the GAA attracts in through the turnstiles, chances are there's nothing drastically wrong with the championships after all. Why doesn't everybody know that?

Eamonn Sweeney
(journalist)

The subsequent torrent of personally abusive comments, tweets and articles is something that I've grown used to. The anonymous letters and phone calls are part of the game now. But you have to keep a sense of perspective. Many others have real-life troubles with ill-health, bereavements and financial worries. We, on the other hand, lost a game of hurling. Passing Dr Morris Park in Thurles on the Monday morning after the game, I saw a couple of hundred kids from around Thurles at the hurling Cúl Camp – hurling away, happy out. Children maybe seven years of age, many of whom had been at the game the day before. They'd moved on by the following morning and were back out hurling. I could hear the shouts and laughter as the different age-group mini games went on. Adults feel the need to stick the boot in; kids seem content in the company of their friends, playing the game that they love.

Lar Corbett
(Tipperary hurler 1998–)

on dealing with defeat to Kilkenny in August 2012

Guys learned very fast that being so absolute in terms of victory and defeat is almost counter-productive and dangerous in ways, psychologically. Balance can be lost, relationships can suffer. After losing an All-Ireland, the emotional wreckage is played out very much off Broadway. The cameras have gone home, the newspapers have stopped writing, about your team at least. In the days after defeats like that, I got the impression the players wanted to be in each other's company more than anyone else, as if no one else understood. It's a difficult time. Random people or even some you know well will come up and offer their opinions, attributing blame in all the places they see fit. It's amazing how strangers think it's okay to cut the legs from under your teammates, close friends. You learn to leave it just go over your head.

Conor McCarthy
(Cork footballer 2004–)

on the trials of losing an All-Ireland final

To play for your country would be anyone's dream. At that time it was daunting. That was in '87, it was compulsory to wear a gum shield. After the first game you realised why it was compulsory.

Stephen King
(Cavan footballer 1981–1997)

The number one philosophy we have in the team is to make the man beside you look better than you, that's the number one rule. When you start thinking that you are above everybody else, that you are more important, that's the day that you are going to pull the team down. We're all equal, it's the men who do the work and try to make the fella beside him look better than them that are really the heart and soul of any team.

Kieran McGeeney
(Armagh footballer 1992–2007, Kildare football manager 2007–)

There is no good in a player being able to cover say twenty or thirty metres very quickly – and let's face it this can be quite a distance to travel with the ball in a high-intensity championship match – if he is going to be very easily robbed of possession by an opponent simply because he does not have the power to withstand the challenge. How often in recent games in the National League have we seen players deprived of hard-won possession because they were unable to resist challenges? Far too often for my liking – it's imperative that we get back to focusing on the basic elements of Gaelic football and one of these most certainly is retaining possession.

Martin McElkennon
(football coach with Derry, Cavan, Tyrone, Monaghan and Meath)

Journalist: So, Nicky what does it mean to win Tipperary's 25th All-Ireland senior hurling title?

Nicky English: It means I'm out of a hole. You take a job like this and you are in a hole from the beginning. People around me, people close to me, when this job came up, they all said don't take it, but I couldn't stop myself taking it. I love Tipperary and the Tipperary hurling jersey so much. I'm very good at digging holes for myself in life anyway. This feels like I've got out of one.

Nicky English
(Tipperary hurler 1982–1996, Tipperary hurling manager 1999–2002)

in the immediate aftermath of guiding Tipperary to the 2001 All-Ireland title

I considered that, no matter how hard or fit or strong or skilful an opponent was, I would eventually get the better of him. There were days when things started happening for me in the last ten minutes of a game, and simply because I would not give in. A championship game is more like a marathon than a sprint and whoever keeps going longest and hardest usually wins out.

Colm O'Rourke
(Meath footballer 1975–1995)

When different lads from different clubs come together they have the huge honour of wearing the county jersey. It's a phenomenal opportunity and a source of pride for them. But the GAA is built on the club, the community and the locality and that's the brilliant thing about it.

Brian Cody
(Kilkenny hurling manager 1998–)

There's such an attachment there with a manager who brings you to All-Ireland success because it's such a long journey and such a difficult journey. Obviously Pat [Gilroy] had a lot of time for me and he developed me so much as a player.

Paul Flynn
(Dublin footballer 2008–)

It's a very emotional thing. People who don't play GAA probably wouldn't understand it and would be asking, 'Well, why are you playing at all?'

Paul Brady
(nine-time All-Ireland handball champion 2003–2012, from Cavan)

on his commitment to his club, Mullahoran, in Cavan

From a personal point of view it's a fantastic experience. That's not just because I'm from a so-called weaker county, it's the same for all players. You look at All-Ireland winners like [Kieran] Donaghy and all these boys like Stevie McDonnell ... they put so much into it as well. It's our only chance to represent our country in what's similar to our sport and it's probably closest to winning an All-Ireland or maybe even an All Star.

Leighton Glynn
(Wicklow footballer 2002–)

on playing in the International Rules series

The best Munster final I ever saw was played in Killarney between Limerick and Tipperary. Of course it wasn't the real thing: you need to see the dust rising around the goalmouth in Thurles.

Con Houlihan
(sports journalist)

They had a phenomenal attitude towards football. If you pulled out of a tackle in Aughawillan, you might as well pack your bags and go. That was it. They built themselves up from zilch. Serious football men.

Declan Darcy
(Leitrim footballer 1988–1998, Dublin footballer 1998–2002)

recalling weekends spent learning about football in his father's parish of Aughawillan, County Leitrim

They have become an inspiration to mid-tier panels like Derry or Armagh, even sleeping giants like Meath and Galway. Because the truly ambitious inter-county squads and managements are forensically examining the Donegal model in order to replicate the glorious success they achieved last month.

Seán Moran
(journalist)

What comes around goes around in football and no team or individual is going to be lucky all the time when it comes to close-run matches and refereeing decisions. Anyone who cannot accept that, no matter how hard it is to swallow on days when there appears to be no justice, is involved in the wrong sport.

Colm O'Rourke
(Meath footballer 1975–1995)

All you see are the two posts and the ball and the opponent standing in front of you with the hands in the air waving. It's just a matter of getting your mind clear, take your five or six paces back and two to the right and set it up and kick it over.

Pádraig Joyce
(Galway footballer 1997–2012)

What do you say about this Kerry team? They're great men. A lot of the talk during the week, writing this team off, served only to fuel the great men in that dressing room. We've been carrying a lot of hurt for the last nine or ten years. We're Kerry at the end of the day. There has been a lot written about this team and a lot of it has been disrespectful. I think today the great men in this team stood up. I'm very proud of that.

Paul Galvin
(Kerry footballer 2003–)

on what it meant for Kerry to finally beat Tyrone in the championship, July 2012

Battle-hardened National League supporters are a more weather-beaten animal than their Championship counterparts.

Eoghan Corry
(journalist)

Club is where you're born and that's where all your memories are. That's where your best friends are; you go to primary school with them, secondary school and even college. I learned all my skills here in the club. We're very passionate about it and in Kilkenny here especially, winning the county final is huge.

Michael Fennelly
(Kilkenny hurler 2003–)

on his club, Ballyhale Shamrocks

You have to be really passionate about a thing if you really truly love it. That's what helps you bring it down to grass roots, because you understand different levels; the players, the referees. If you don't have that true feel for it then it doesn't come across and I truly love it.

Aileen Lawlor
(Camogie Association President 2012–)

I can always remember wandering into it afterwards and the lads asking where the bus was parked and the manager Billy Morgan going, 'No, the fecking bus is gone, we're walking down because we've never experienced this before', and it was the greatest moment of all because as the players walked through the town we realised how important it was to the people, and the joy of the supporters to finally come across the border and beat the Kingdom comprehensively. It was the start of a great team.

Larry Tompkins
(Kildare footballer 1979–1985 and Cork footballer 1987–1996)

on beating Kerry 0–13 to 1–05, in the 1987 Munster final

I remember kicking that point and the crowd going crazy. I remember being seven points down and the substitutes that we put in all clicking. I remember Andy Moran's goal. But my biggest memory is giving an absolutely brutal pass that Darren Magee cut out. The ball went down to the far corner of the Canal End and I said to myself, 'Here we go again.' It went out for a forty-five, a combination of Clarkey [goalkeeper David Clarke] and David Brady punched it out. It just shows the thin line from one second being totally elated to making an absolute mess of things a minute later.

Ciarán McDonald
(Mayo footballer 1994–2007)

recalling the 2006 All-Ireland semi-final between Dublin and Mayo

Séamus Coleman was probably as good a Gaelic footballer as I have ever seen playing at his age. Brilliant. Séamus Coleman was a centre-half back. He reminded me of Kevin Moran, a young Kevin Moran. It's interesting that he has made it as well. When I saw him playing for Killybegs, he reminded me of Kevin Moran.

Martin McHugh
(Donegal footballer 1981–1994)

on Everton star Séamus Coleman's early days as a promising Gaelic footballer with Killybegs in Donegal

I wouldn't leave a football field until I had every-thing perfected. I always have this thing, even in matches, that I would have to score the last kick I kick. I can't leave on a miss. I always have to leave on a good note. That's one superstition I have.

Ciarán Kilkenny
(Dublin footballer 2012–)

It isn't really until later on, when you see the amount of brilliant teams and brilliant players that never achieved it or never won an All-Ireland final, that you realise it. The regrets of having missed out on that must be very big. We class ourselves as very lucky in that sense and I suppose it's a great honour to look back and be able to say that you achieved that. To be on a team that won an All-Ireland final is an exceptional thing. It puts you in an exceptional category really.

Conor Hayes
(Galway hurler 1979–1989, Galway hurling manager 2002–2006)

Gaelic football is like a love affair. If you don't take it seriously it's no fun, if you do take it seriously, it will break your heart.

Patrick Kavanagh
(poet and Monaghan man)

I'm a realistic person and I know if GAA was professional I wouldn't be in Australia in a million years.

Setanta Ó hAilpín
(Cork hurler 2003, Australian Rules footballer with Carlton Football Club 2005–2011)

Traditionally Kerry have always been a catch and kick team. Going back to the 1970s and 1980s I think Kerry were always kicking ball. I think it is bred into us. I think most people in Kerry are advocates of kicking the ball. I don't think there are too many coaches below in Kerry who are interested in hand-passing the ball, so hopefully we will continue with that.

Colm 'Gooch' Cooper
(Kerry footballer 2000–)

We wanted guys who could work, and work really hard. We were amazed at the reaction we got from the players. The harder it got and the more work that was done with them, the more they wanted it. We have to say that the success is down to the players really. Maybe over the years Galway had a lot of skilful players and had shown a lot of credentials at minor level. But they have now turned this around into big performances and that was the most rewarding thing for us.

Anthony Cunningham
(Galway hurling manager 2012–)

I believe you can manifest the things you want in your life, if you've got the right mental attitude and a bit of positivity.

Paul Galvin
(Kerry footballer 2003–)

More so than anything, it's the team element that can't be overstated. No matter where you go there's always someone, somewhere, from some team sport, and it's just a buzz that's hard to beat.

Mattie Forde
(Wexford footballer 1999–2011)

Success is different things to different people. For some people it's playing in Croke Park on All-Ireland final day, for others it's being able to compete at inter-county level and maintain the number of girls that are playing at U12 and still having those girls playing at adult level – that too is success and is vital to the lifeblood of the game.

Mary O'Connor
(Cork camogie and football player 1996–2009 and National Director of Camogie Development)

This wasn't so much a Wexford All-Ireland final. This was an Irish people's All-Ireland. This was giving people back belief that we can do it. You see the GAA is more than just an organisation that plays sport. The GAA is the very root of our culture. It's the root of who we are.

George O'Connor
(Wexford hurler 1979–1996)

commenting on Wexford's victory in the 1996 All-Ireland final

A solid television promotion would also increase the sports' popularity in China. If we can get our TV campaign tidied up abroad and actually publicise our games then I think there would be a huge take-up in China because China is supposed to be the place where ball and stick games originated.

Liam O'Neill
(GAA President 2012–)

The most important thing for us is the thirty-man squad we have, the backroom team we have. For us, representing Donegal is a massive, massive honour. Jim [McGuinness] always refers to it before we go out onto a football pitch and we put on our Donegal jerseys, that we are not just representing ourselves but that we are representing the whole county and when we pull off the jersey, we are still representatives of Donegal. That's very important for us, whether that be in Dublin at a pre- or post-match meal, whether that be speaking to media, we are conscious that we are representing Donegal and it is important that we uphold that tradition.

Michael Murphy
(Donegal footballer 2007–)

He's had a serious career for a long time, over-coming serious injuries. But when I talk about Henry, he was outstanding, but he's the ulti-mate team player and his intent, always, is to in-fluence the game for the benefit of the team. It's not about him scoring phenomenal amounts, though he's capable of doing that, it's the work-rate he showed in the second half which was key to the whole thing. It doesn't worry me who picks it up and drives it on, but it's the team, the team, the team. It's the panel, the whole thing, and all you ask of everybody is that they try their best.

Brian Cody

(Kilkenny hurling manager 1998–)

on Henry Shefflin's second-half performance in the All-Ireland final, 2012

I've always said that the levels of commitment in Gaelic are extraordinary. Rugby players are well paid for what they do but, because they are paid, they have the time to commit completely to what they do. But professionalism is a state of mind. It's about applying yourself to the nth degree and just because the amateurs, in a sense, don't get paid, it doesn't preclude them from the professional approach. I think the level of work and energy and commitment that the GAA players make to their sport is extraordinary.

Eddie O'Sullivan
(Irish rugby team manager 2001–2008)

We took so long to perfect Plan A that there simply wasn't time for Plan B. Anyway, what happens if Plan B doesn't work?

Joe Kernan
(Armagh footballer 1971–1988, Armagh football manager 2001–2006)

The best experience I ever had coaching was in Limavady College, when there was no Gaelic football team when I went up there and I had to try and get a team together, and we won the league in the first year, won a championship in the second year and there was a young lad that never played the game before and he came on in the final in the second year for about five minutes and he won the ball, dropped the ball. Then a couple of minutes after that he won the ball again, slipped it to someone else who kicked it over the bar. That was the best buzz I ever got out of football coaching, because this young fella never set foot on a pitch before and all of a sudden, on a very small level, he was part of a winning team and his face and his teammates' faces looking at him were absolutely unbelievable after the game.

Jim McGuinness
(Donegal football manager 2010–)

The real hurling guy will see the other sides of a lad's play. The guys who know nothing about hurling see you scoring and scoring, but the real hurling man will see you making a run to the corner, maybe holding up the play, maybe being a bit more physical and the ball spilling off you for other guys to come on to.

Eoin Kelly
(Tipperary hurler 2000–)

You have to focus on what every game is. You can't just be looking to an All-Ireland final, you can't be thinking two games ahead to a Munster final. It's about respect to the game you're playing. Every other team is training hard and trying to get better so your own game will suffer if you don't apply that focus. That's stood to us and a lot of Kerry fellas in the past.

Marc Ó Sé
(Kerry footballer 2002–)

The game was back in Austin Stack Park and it was tight. In the closing stages of the game I shipped a dead leg for my troubles. But my heart was pumping on my sleeve. Adrenaline, endorphins or whatever keeps you from lying down, I had 'em, I refused to buckle. As we entered the closing stages we trailed by a point again and this time I fisted the equaliser. Extra time. Anyone who has ever experienced a game like this can understand what the atmosphere was like. It may be a small, insignificant sporting event, but it is the GAA at its most beautiful. Local, bitter, passionate, courageous.

Páidí Ó Sé

(Kerry footballer 1975–1987, Kerry football manager 1996–2003, Westmeath manager 2004–2006, Clare manager 2006)

describes the closing stages of a Kerry schoolboy game between the St Michael's, Listowel, and the Sem., Killarney, in 1974

I suppose what I would find about playing further out the field is the ball handling. Being able to become part of the play, and it will help me to link up with defenders and improve me that way. That would be a major advantage in that regard. It helps with the kick-outs too.

Paul Durcan
(Donegal football goalkeeper 2004–)
on the benefits to a goalkeeper of playing outfield occasionally

Mental conditioning is similar to physical conditioning. At four to six weeks you can see a marked difference in confidence, in composure, in leadership, in concentration only if, and it's a big if, you put the same amount of time and effort into it as you do in your physical conditioning.

Enda McNulty
(Armagh footballer 1996–2010)

Ireland would be a pretty barren place without it; the GAA is the pulse of the people of Ireland. Whether it be Owenmore Gaels in Collooney in Sligo or St Vincent's in Dublin, it is the GAA that have put in the infrastructure for the young people of Ireland. They are the epicentre of the local community. I know that there's money coming from Lotto and indeed from Croke Park, but essentially it's the people themselves who have done it.

Marty Morrissey
(GAA commentator)

There's such a thing as hurling fitness. And there's physical fitness. You must combine both. You'll get fellows who can hurl all day but they couldn't hurl at pace, which is very important.

Justin McCarthy
(Cork hurler 1964–1974, Waterford hurling manager 2001–2008)

If you're not able to compete physically, then you're not going to compete in football. It's as simple as that. But likewise, even if you're in very good shape physically but aren't in good shape football-wise, you're not going to be able to compete at the top end either. That hasn't changed. It's just now there's a little more detail known about what the actual game is like. It's a stop-start game, the same as any other field sport. There's no need to be running marathons as I would have myself with the club coming up through the ranks.

Barry Solan
(physical trainer to many of the leading GAA teams and players)

Their best asset is their collective engine. They are a tremendously fit group of footballers. I hear stories about the intensity of McGuinness's training sessions. It is all based on small-sided football games. Starting with four on four, to eight on eight, to twelve on twelve, with no quarter given and non-stop for ninety minutes.

John O'Keefe
(Kerry footballer 1969–1984)

on 2012 All-Ireland champions Donegal

It's not the colours of the jerseys that will count. It's the fifteen Down men on the pitch who can make all the difference. I'm not in the least superstitious. You must put all such nonsense to one side and play to your full potential.

Benny Coulter
(Down footballer 2000–)

on wearing alternate colours for the 2010 All-Ireland football final at Croke Park

At Nemo we try to give all the kids a game and bring them along. We're not too worried about winning underage titles. Sometimes you have to take off your best players to give the other lads a chance. The young fella who is only barely getting his game at fourteen can turn into a star at twenty-one.

Billy Morgan
(Cork hurler and footballer 1966–1981 and Cork football manager 1986–1996, 2003–2007)

on the Nemo Rangers club training philosophy

Of course there's a mountain of commitment that's needed to be a modern-day inter-county footballer or hurler, but it's an honour to represent your county.

Darran O'Sullivan
(Kerry footballer 2005–)

I actually love going out on wet and windy nights, turning up to go training, because you don't have anything else in your head and you are devoting those two hours to the training.

Oisín McConville
(Armagh footballer 1994–2008)

This is a great day for Irish sport and a decision to be welcomed by everyone involved with Irish sport. I have always dreamed of playing at Croke Park and I am delighted that I could get the chance now. I never got the chance to play Gaelic football there and I have always wanted to play at Croke Park. Who wouldn't?

Brian O'Driscoll
(Leinster and Ireland rugby player 1999–)

on the news that Croke Park would be made available for international rugby matches

Today above all, it is in a positive spirit that we welcome Your Majesty and Your Royal Highness to Croke Park. Your presence does honour to our Association, to its special place in Irish life, and to its hundreds of thousands of members. Today will go down in the history of the Gaelic Athletic Association.

Christy Cooney
(GAA President 2009–2012)

addressing Queen Elizabeth II of Great Britain when she visited Croke Park in May 2011

If one guy is scared, you're probably not going to win, because the margins are that tight. It's very difficult to get thirty guys really believing that they can win these massive ball games.

Liam McHale
(Mayo footballer 1988–2001)

Whenever you fail a test you can bury your head in the sand and pretend it never happened. Or you can get up and try to do something about it. At the time, it might seem like the worst thing that ever happened to you, but the harder you work the more sense the challenge you faced seems to make. I got up after a big fall and I've never looked back.

Jim Stynes
(Dublin minor footballer 1983–1984 and Australian Rules footballer with Melbourne Football Club 1987–1998)

Journalist: How's the leg Kevin?

Kevin Moran: It's fuc … it's very sore.

Television interview with the Dublin footballer, later Irish international soccer player, Kevin Moran, after the 1978 All-Ireland final against Kerry

It's just good practice, that's all, and it applies at every level. The information is all there. The right fuels are there. It's like anything else – if you're driving a high-performance car you need the right fuel and enough of it, and if it's not there the car simply won't perform. That's the reason there is such an emphasis now on proper hydration and proper nutrition.

Dessie Dolan
(Westmeath footballer 1999–)

The important thing for the free-taker is to block everything out – the noise, the nerves, the various decisions you might make.

Johnny Dooley
(Offaly hurler 1991–2002)

Anyway, there's not a whole lot that needs to be changed with this Kerry team. We don't need to reinvent the wheel. We're just going to have to become fitter, stronger, more tactically aware, better organised and maybe a bit more cynical. But the ingredients are still there. That's why the winter will be fun, trying to come up with ways to take on the Donegals, Mayos, Dublins and Corks. I can't wait for training to start.

Kieran Donaghy
(Kerry footballer 2004–)

When you want to win a game you have to be able to adjust your game plan when it suits.

Mick O'Dowd
(Meath football manager 2012–)

The toughest match I ever attended was between Inniskeen and Donaghmoyne. The exchanges from the beginning were fierce, with players being felled all over the place. It was ten minutes before any of the players noticed the referee had not thrown the ball in.

Patrick Kavanagh
(poet and Monaghan man)

Nah, I don't bother practising them too much – I just hit them on the day. It is a bit of a responsibility, especially in tight games. The ball is the most important thing and you have to keep your focus and make sure you get a good strike on it. You have to just hope that you get a strike on it and that the goalkeeper doesn't guess the right way and that it goes in.

Stephen O'Neill
(Tyrone footballer 1999–)
on the art of scoring penalties

I started doing yoga last year and I found it great. If you do yoga for an hour and a half, it's harder than any training session. You'd probably do more stretching there than you would in six months of training.

Trevor Mortimer
(Mayo footballer 2000–2012)

I got ambushed, I was on my way to the game when about forty Donegal fans invited me in. It brings back a lot of very happy memories from my childhood coming here, so I'm really looking forward to it.

Neil Lennon
(Glasgow Celtic soccer club manager 2010–)
on his way into Croke Park before the 2012 All-Ireland final

Whatever jersey we don, whatever team we support, our parishes, our communities and our lives have been transformed by the positive influences of the Gaelic Athletic Association. It is indeed no exaggeration to say that 127 years after its foundation, the Association forms an intrinsic part of the fabric of Irish society.

Enda Kenny TD
(Taoiseach 2011–)

It's a huge disappointment when the team loses. It affects the whole family. There is literally a depression. People not involved in the sport wouldn't understand that.

Sinéad Dooley
(wife of Johnny Dooley, Offaly hurler 1991–2002)

You can talk these things over too much while preparing for the big games. The only place to do your talking is the on the pitch.

Anthony Tohill
(Derry footballer 1991–2003 and Ireland International Rules team manager 2010–2011)

A fan is someone who, if you have made an idiot of yourself on the pitch, doesn't think you've done a permanent job.

Jack Lynch
(Cork footballer and hurler 1936–1950, Taoiseach 1966–1973, 1977–1979)

I keep some sheep myself, so when I want to relax I head away up the hill away from everything. I'm into the two businesses that don't pay – sheep and football!

Michael Hegarty
(Donegal footballer 1999–2012)

I never got hit by a car or anything, like, but it certainly feels as close as you could get to it.

Davy Fitzgerald
(Clare hurling goalkeeper 1990–2008, Waterford hurling manager 2008–2011, Clare hurling manager 2011–)

on losing the All-Ireland hurling final to Kilkenny in 2008

There's no doubt about it. A couple of years ago, I wouldn't have been one to love or even enjoy training, but this past two or three years going to training has been brilliant and I have cherished every game I play. I know there mightn't be too many more seasons left as an inter-county player and you do appreciate it more and enjoy it more.

Benny Coulter
(Down footballer 2000–)

I love hearing stories about teams in the 1950s, 1960s and 1970s, the Christy Rings and all that. It fascinates me, because to understand where you are going in the future you need to know about the past.

Seán Óg Ó hAilpín
(Cork hurler 1995–2012)

Momentum is great, especially with a young team, because winning is a habit just as much as losing is a habit.

Nicky Quaid
(Limerick hurler 2010–)

That's been a big, big thing for this group of players, not to quit, to stay going, stay chasing, stay working hard and stay honest.

Tom Helebert
(Galway hurling selector 2012)

There are always times when you think 'Feck it, I'm in no form for this' and when you wish you weren't training – but it's when you are not training that you realise how much you want to be out there working on your game and improving.

Darran O'Sullivan
(Kerry footballer 2005–)

April arrived with an air of hope and optimism. I like that month; the slate is clean, winter is over and it's a time when you can sense the hard work starting to pay off and it signals the start of the real business in the GAA world.

Liam Dunne
(Wexford hurler 1988–2003)

All I knew was playing the games and maybe people thought I was boring, just training and matches, but I loved it.

Seán Óg Ó hAilpín
(Cork hurler 1995–2012)

This team we are coaching will play flat-out, high-tempo football with a complete emphasis on skill. We are trying to make them a kicking team. We want them to be the cleverest team of all time with the ball in hand. And we have been working on that day in and day out. Our theme is: the ball, the ball, the ball.

Kevin McStay
(Mayo footballer 1983–1990 and football analyst)

on his coaching philosophy for St Brigid's of Roscommon, the All-Ireland club champions 2013

I think you can do a lot of very productive work with players in a session lasting fifty minutes. The emphasis now should be not just on keeping them sharp, but ensuring that their pace and power are applied to team strategy – in terms of support play, offloading the ball sharply, making quick breaks to create space and, crucially, retaining the ball in the tackle. Why would you want to put players through the mill when the ball is actually only in play during a typical game for about twenty-four minutes? I would contend that a lot of training being done at the minute is counterproductive.

Martin McElkennon
(football coach with Derry, Cavan, Tyrone,
Monaghan and Meath)

If two poor teams are on the pitch and one is much fitter, that team will win.

Kevin Heffernan
(Dublin footballer 1948–1962, Dublin football manager 1973–1976 and 1979–1983)

A No. 3 who fails to assert himself is on his way to being No. 23.

Mick Lyons
(Meath footballer 1979–1992)

Football is more than football. It is about character. What you do on the field reflects what you feel about things. It is guys who will give everything, who will absolutely open themselves out, to show themselves to you. To show themselves to their comrades.

Tommy Carr
(Dublin footballer 1985–1993)

The primary responsibility for a forward is to do the right thing for the team; so if you get ten balls in a match and you go for ten scores but they weren't the right option then you are letting the team down.

Lar Corbett
(Tipperary hurler 1998–)

As much won't do. You have to give more every year. That's the way it's gone.

Pádraig Joyce
(Galway footballer 1997–2012)

Some people say hurling isn't very important in the scheme of things. But to hurling people, hurling *is* the scheme of things.

Ger Loughnane
(Clare hurler 1973–1987, Clare hurling manager 1994–2000, Galway manager 2006–2008)

You say to me that there is more to life than hurling. Well if you want to carry on like a fella who is not an inter-county hurler, well then there will be more to life than hurling. Lots more. But there won't be hurling. That's the reality of it.

Brian Cody
(Kilkenny hurling manager 1998–)

The Kerry supporter is very demanding and I think that what makes Kerry football great is that we are a very demanding county with regard to our football; we constantly want success and that's fine. I wouldn't want it any other way.

Éamonn Fitzmaurice
(Kerry footballer 1998–2006, Kerry football manager 2012–)

Play as much as you can, when you can and above all, look, listen and learn. Practice does make perfect, but you can also learn so much by watching players on TV, or better still, going to see them play in the flesh.

Graham Geraghty
(Meath footballer 1991–2012)
with advice for young players

To young players of today I would say to practise the skills of the game as often as possible. I used to hit a tennis ball off the gable end wall of our house in Midleton and the countless hours spent in this way helped in no small way in later years.

John Fenton
(Cork hurler 1975–1987)

Positive language doesn't guarantee positive results, but negative language will guarantee defeats.

Mickey Harte
(Tyrone football manager 2003–)

The majority of consensus would be that once you reach thirty in sport you are finished, you're gone, which is crude and harsh. What you do on the pitch and around training does have a knock-on effect. But it's your lifestyle outside of training that is the key to sustaining a prolonged career.

Seán Óg Ó hAilpín
(Cork hurler 1995–2012)

The local paper stated we were all Trojans in defence and wizards in attack. I once got a lot of kudos from a report which described me as 'incisive around goal'. No one knew the meaning of the word incisive, but it sounded good.

Patrick Kavanagh
(poet and Monaghan man)

in his famous essay 'Gut Yer Man'

Here's a free piece of advice from somebody who used to know. There is only one way to teach a forward to kick the ball over the bar. It is called practice.

Pat Spillane
(Kerry footballer 1975–1991, GAA analyst)

It's been a childhood dream to play for Dublin for the last ten years, but time to go. It was a great journey and I loved every second.

Tomás 'Mossy' Quinn
(Dublin footballer 2003–2012)

on his retirement from inter-county football

One thing about punditry, which is funny, is that you're never wrong. If you're wrong on the Friday, you can backtrack by the Monday. When you're playing, if you're wrong on the Sunday then you're guaranteed to get it in the neck on Monday. So it's an easier lifestyle in many ways, but it doesn't beat or even match that buzz of playing at Croke Park.

Ciarán Whelan
(Dublin footballer 1996–2009 and football analyst)

The Dodger has it. The Dodger is moving in. A shot from the Dodger and it's gone over the bar – another point for Kilkenny. In case you came in from Mars today, the Dodger is D. J. Carey of Gowran and Kilkenny.

Micheál Ó Muircheartaigh
(legendary GAA commentator)

It was a great medal to get. I had the honour and the pleasure that year of captaining a great bunch of lads. We haven't looked back since.

John Mullane
(Waterford hurler 2001–2012)

on winning his first ever championship medal with his club, De La Salle, in 2008

BIBLIOGRAPHY

Boylan, Seán & Quinn, John (2006). *Seán Boylan: The Will to Win*. The O'Brien Press.

Breheny, Michael & Keenan, Donal (2001). *The Ultimate Encyclopedia of Gaelic Football and Hurling*. Carlton Books.

Breheny, Martin & Keys, Colm (2004). *The Chosen Ones: Celebrating 1000 GAA All Stars*. Blackwater Press.

Cahill, Jackie (2005). *Passion and Pride: The Official Biography of Davy Fitzgerald*. Blackwater Press.

Carter, Charlie & McEvoy, Enda (2005). *Triumph and Troubles: The Official Biography of Charlie Carter*. Blackwater Press.

Cody, Brian & Breheny, Martin (2009). *Cody: The Autobiography*. Irish Sports Publishing.

Corry, Eoghan (2005). *An Illustrated History of the GAA*. Gill & Macmillan.

Corry, Eoghan (2011). *Deadlock: Dublin vs Meath 1991*. Gill & Macmillan.

Cronin, Mike, Duncan, Mark & Rouse, Paul (2009). *The GAA: A People's History*. The Collins Press.

Cusack, Dónal Óg (2009). *Come What May: The autobiography*. Penguin Ireland.

Dunne, Liam & Lawlor, Damian (2004). *I Crossed the Line: The Liam Dunne Story*. Sliabh Bán Productions.

Farrell, Dessie & Potts, Seán (2005). *Tangled Up in Blue*. TownHouse.

Fullam, Brendan (2011). *Decades of Stars: A Collection of Hurling Heroes*. Orpen Press Limited.

Griffin, Jane (2001) *Food for Sport, Eat Well, Perform Better*. Crowood.

Hayes, Liam (2010). *Out of Our Skins: An autobiography* (20th Anniversary Edition). Blackwater Press.

Horgan, Tim (2009). *Christy Ring: Hurling's Greatest*. The Collins Press.

Houlihan, Con (2003). *More than a Game: Selected Sporting Essays*. Liberties Press.

Keating, Michael & Keenan, Donal (1996). *Babs – A legend in Irish Sport: The Michael Keating Story.* Storm Books.

Kennelly, Tadhg (2009). *Tadhg Kennelly: Unfinished Business.* Mercier Press.

McCarthy, Finbarr (2009). *Bainisteoir: The 10 Greatest GAA Managers.* Mentor Books.

McEvoy, Enda (2012). *The Godfather of Modern Hurling: The Father Tommy Maher Story.* Ballpoint Press.

McNaughton, Terence (1998). *Sambo: All or Nothing.* Wolfhound Press.

McRory, Séamus (2005). *The All-Ireland Dream: Over 25 interviews with GAA Greats.* Wolfhound Press.

O'Connor, Philip (2011). *A Parish Far From Home: How Gaelic Football Brought the Irish in Stockholm Together.* Gill & Macmillan.

Ó hAnnracháin, Eoghan & Davey, Cathal (2008). *More than a Sporting Experience: 30 Years of Gaelic Games in Luxembourg.* Gaelic Sports Club Luxembourg.

Ó hEithir, Breandán (1984). *Over the Bar: A Personal Relationship with the GAA*. Ward River Press.

Ó Muircheartaigh, Micheál (2004). *From Dún Síon to Croke Park*. Penguin Ireland.

Ó Muircheartaigh, Micheál, McKeon, Conor & Potts, Seán (2009). *Micheál's GAA Odyssey: A Celebration of Gaelic Games*. Mainstream Publishing.

O'Rourke, Colm (1996). *The Final Whistle*. Hero Books Limited.

O'Sullivan, Éamon (1958). *The Art and Science of Gaelic Football*. The Kerryman.

Spillane, Pat & McGoldrick, Sean (1998). *Shooting from the Hip: The Pat Spillane Story*. Storm Books.

MERCIER PRESS

IRISH PUBLISHER - IRISH STORY

We hope you enjoyed this book.

Since 1944, Mercier Press has published books that have been critically important to Irish life and culture. Books that dealt with subjects that informed readers about Irish scholars, Irish writers, Irish history and Ireland's rich heritage.

We believe in the importance of providing accessible histories and cultural books for all readers and all who are interested in Irish cultural life.

Our website is the best place to find out more information about Mercier, our books, authors, news and the best deals on a wide variety of books. Mercier tracks the best prices for our books online and we seek to offer the best value to our customers.

Sign up on our website to receive updates and special offers.

www.mercierpress.ie
www.facebook.com/mercier.press
www.twitter.com/irishpublisher

Mercier Press, Unit 3b, Oak House, Bessboro Rd, Blackrock, Cork, Ireland